D0879769

the Green
museum

MAY 2 1 2010

MINNESOTA STATE UNIVERSITY LIBRARY
MANKATO, MN 56002-8419

the Green museum

A Primer on Environmental Practice

Sarah S. Brophy and Elizabeth Wylie

ALTAMIRA
PRESS

A Division of
ROWMAN & LITTLEFIELD PUBLISHERS, INC.
Lanham • New York • Toronto • Plymouth, UK

ALTAMIRA PRESS
A division of Rowman & Littlefield Publishers, Inc.
A wholly owned subsidiary of The Rowman & Littlefield Pu~~blishing Group~~, Inc.
4501 Forbes Boulevard, Suite 200
Lanham, MD 20706
www.altamirapress.com

AM
7
.B765
2008

Estover Road
Plymouth PL6 7PY
United Kingdom

Copyright © 2008 by AltaMira Press

All rights reserved. No part of this publication may be reproduced, stored in a retrieval system, or transmitted in any form or by any means, electronic, mechanical, photocopying, recording, or otherwise, without the prior permission of the publisher.

British Library Cataloguing in Publication Information Available

Library of Congress Cataloging-in-Publication Data

Brophy, Sarah S., 1961–
    The green museum : a primer on environmental practice / Sarah S. Brophy and Elizabeth Wylie.
        p. cm.   7057602
    ISBN-13: 978-0-7591-1164-6 (cloth : alk. paper)
    ISBN-10: 0-7591-1164-2 (cloth : alk. paper)
    ISBN-13: 978-0-7591-1165-3 (pbk. : alk. paper)
    ISBN-10: 0-7591-1165-0 (pbk. : alk. paper)
    ISBN 13: 978-07591-1225-4 (electronic)
    ISBN 10: 0-7591-1225-8 (electronic)
    1. Museums—Environmental aspects—Handbooks, manuals, etc. 2. Sustainable design—Handbooks, manuals, etc. 3. Environmentalism—Handbooks, manuals, etc. 4. Museum techniques—Handbooks, manuals, etc. 5. Museums—Management—Handbooks, manuals, etc. I.Wylie, Elizabeth. II. Title.
    AM7.B765 2008
    069—dc22   2008008230

Printed in the United States of America

∞™ The paper used in this publication meets the minimum requirements of American National Standard for Information Sciences—Permanence of Paper for Printed Library Materials, ANSI/NISO Z39.48–1992.

Contents

Figures and Tables

Acknowledgments

WE HAVE talked to so many contributors to the green museum movement: architects, engineers, museum professionals, and funders. What has been so exciting for us is the opportunity to pull together all this wonderful work and acknowledge it all in one place so that others can learn from their collective experiences. Many have contributed to the making of this book and we have tried to acknowledge everyone who has shared their experiences and expertise. We are frustrated that we could not include everyone's contributions, or institutions, in the text, but we are very, very grateful for their time and interest.

Sarah particularly wishes to thank Tim McNeil of the Design Museum, who is her exhibition guru and provided much of the material for that section; Julie Silverman of ECHO for so very many great ideas and examples; and Bill Gilmore of Chesapeake Bay Maritime Museum, who is her energy efficiency guru and go-to guy for all sorts of facilities issues. Elizabeth especially thanks her former colleagues at HKT Architects for being a helpful resource, and she also honors her son, Spencer Cheek, for inspiring deep thought about the environmental legacy we are leaving for him and his children, and in turn their children.

Ellie Altman
Sandra Ambrozy
John Amodeo
Sam Anderson
Barbara Applebaum
Maud Ayson
Ana Bacall
Barbra Batshalom

Patsy Benviniste
Juliette M. Bianco
Aaron Binkley
Bob Brais
James Bulloch
John Castle
Ellen Censky
Sue Chin

David Coleman
Greg Dennis
Robert Forloney
Damien Francaviglia
Patrice Frey
Michael Furbish
Gavin Gardi
Bill Gillmore
Vicki Greene
Jen Gresham
Victoria Grossman
Bill Hammer
Paul Himmelstein
Nancy Hughes
Ronald L. Hurst
John Jacobsen
Michelle Jost
Eric Kluz
Mary Lou Krambeer
Joan Krevlin
John Krueger
Susan Lacerte
John Linehan
Joseph Matyas
Joseph May
Tim McNeil
Ruth Newell
David Overholt
Bonnie Paganis
Stuart Parnes
Gioia Perugini

Ken Peterson
Richard Piacentini
Jack Plumb
Bob Prescott
Kurt Reisweber
Laura Roberts
Tanya Salvey
Chris Schaffner
Chris Sheppard
Sheila Sheridan
Matthew Siegal
Patty Silence
Julie Silverman
Gene Slear
Janet Slemenda
Mitchel Smith
Steve Smith
Gail Stavitsky
Rick Stockwood
Randall Stout
Nancy Stueber
Brian Thomson
David Uschold
Claudia Vietch
Stu Weinreb
David Wildfire
Mary Tod Winchester
David Winfield
Meg Winikates
Jim Younger

Introduction

A S PROFESSIONALS trained in art history and history, we are unabashed museum people with a collective forty-four years in the field. The idea that this book would be useful to the museum community has been driven home countless times as we talked to other museum people all over the country: the art museum director in Vermont who thought green and collections care did not mix; the paleontologist in Oklahoma who, as head of his museum's green team, was unsure about the best replacement for their café's Styrofoam cups; the objects conservator who is frustrated by lack of attention to air quality outside the museum; the CFO in New Jersey who is astounded by the rapid rise in the museum's utility bills.

As we attended American Association of Museums conferences and others, we talked to more folks who also expressed an urgency about addressing environmental practices in their museums; an urgency about wanting to do something; and an urgency about stepping up to make sure their institution was seen as doing something. Green is one of those things—once you catch it, understand it, and see the very real need for collective action around climate change and environmental issues—you see it everywhere. It is much like learning a new word and henceforth you hear it once a day.

Take water for example. Lately we have been hearing a lot about water as the Southeast struggles with severe drought, and as climate models forecast shortages in the Southwest, the area with the fastest-growing population centers. Some say water is the new oil; some call it liquid gold. Across the country, increasingly strict water usage regulations on the municipal, state and regional, and national levels cannot help but impact aquariums, whose dependency on water is critical to collections care. What about botanical gardens whose species protection plans require water? What about heritage gardens? They use water and plenty of it to maintain historic land-scapes that speak to our cultural heritage and offer places for beauty and relaxation. Let's then consider our rivers, streams, lakes, and coastlines whose ecological systems sustain the very flora and fauna, and support the historic sites and lifeways museums are trying to preserve and interpret. How are museums' building and operational practices negatively affecting those environments?

How about energy use? Worldwide, energy production is responsible for threatening our collective heritage and ecology. Monuments and historic places, buildings and artifacts, are being degraded and destroyed by energy production and pollution from industrialization. Animal and flora species are being lost. What about light pollution and the mission activities of planetariums? What about land planning? How do sprawl and the loss of open space affect the mission of a natural history museum and its ability to carry out field studies? Dig sites are disturbed and overrun; migration routes and habitat are disrupted. Should museums be contributing to these outcomes?

What about air quality? Folks involved in collections care worry about air quality. Why? Consider the painting that was permanently pockmarked because the bubbles in the bubble wrap had trapped pollution that migrated to the painting surface. Paintings are one thing, but what about people? Payroll is usually the largest budget item at any museum. Indoor environmental quality (thermal comfort, as well as lighting and air quality) has huge impacts on productivity and the health and wellness of the staff, not to mention the comfort of visitors and volunteers. What about educational missions and the data that support increases in learning levels in green environments? What about the children's museum whose carpets, adhesives, and cleaning practices might be contributing to asthma in its vulnerable school-age audience? Not convinced? How about studies that show sales increase by 40 percent with the introduction of daylighting into retail environments?

We live on the Maryland Eastern Shore and in Boston, and are aware of our communities' special geographically based concerns about environmental issues. On vacation travels to Florida, New Mexico, and elsewhere we have tuned in to regional concerns around energy, water, and our collective future. We also, like you for sure, have been reading the newspapers. Practically every day there is a story about something linked to environmental issues and climate change, new data about it, or consequences of it. Cartographers are having a hard time keeping up with changes in shorelines as erosion continues apace. Major fashion manufacturers have hired climatologists as the sales cycle for winter clothing has shifted and there is less demand for heavy coats. Loss of farm animal breeds worldwide is a real concern as mass food production has pushed out small farmers. Now there is "doom tourism," a rush to visit endangered places like the Great Barrier Reef and Patagonian glaciers before they are gone. One could go on.

This book is based on the experiences and knowledge of scores of people who are already greening museums. We wanted to gather this information as a primer—a beginning for folks who want to green their institutions too. Mindful of the paleontologist struggling with Styrofoam cups, we wanted to point the way by sharing best practices, stories of innovation and creativity, and resources. We also recognize that most museums are not mega-institutions with huge capital projects underway. Rather, most are small to medium sized. Few have full- or even part-time facilities managers, never mind sustainability officers. This book is for all museums.

How many full-paying visitors does it take to pay your annual electric bill? Try the math—it could be thousands of visitors, couldn't it? Think what else you would rather buy with admissions income—staff time, collections materials, program opportunities? As museum professionals we are desperate to help institutions find money and ways to integrate with their communities and fulfill their missions, while also helping the environment.

We want to encourage museums to reconcile old behaviors and new opportunities by showing the field what good green work is already happening. The danger is that this sort of discussion can get very preachy very quickly. But guilt is not our intent; sharing information and promoting learning and thoughtful decision making are what this book is about. You will make your own choices; we want you to make informed ones.

We would also like to say that no one person can know it all or do it all. The field is changing so rapidly, and new discoveries are coming at such a pace, that it can easily be overwhelming. Do your own research. Talk to peers and colleagues; plug into industry associations; and of course use the Internet. The field is evolving as we write these words and no one solution will fit every institution. Your best defense is a good offense: read, learn, explore, and collaborate. That is the natural habitat for a museum person, isn't it?

We are not architects, engineers, lighting specialists, or facilities managers. We are trained in the humanities, and not of a particularly technical bent of mind. Yet we have tried to learn from others, have read a lot, and present technical information here with a grain of salt. We confess we struggled with some technical details and relied on friendly experts to help sort them out for us.

And we have some other confessions: Sarah still loves a long hot shower, uses a clothes dryer sometimes, and lets her son drive hours each week for soccer practice. She has, however, moved her family to a community where nearly everything (but soccer) is within walking distance, and they are trying to survive with one car. She has always recycled and used both sides of recycled paper; now she composts and has vowed not to buy new material to cut up to make into quilts.

Elizabeth loves a road trip, has a leaky building envelope on her 1905 house, and used way too much paper in the course of researching and writing this book. She, like Sarah, has always recycled, now no longer buys plastic-bottled water, and vows her next car will be a fuel-efficient hybrid. Everyone comes to environmentally sustainable practices from their own set of circumstances, abilities, and level of knowledge.

Armed with the knowledge that many in our field already recognize the threat of climate change and are responding to the best of their abilities, doesn't it make sense that you and your museum should too?

Where there is a will there is a way. So many museums want to (and can) be leaders and teachers in the move toward a more environmentally sustainable future for our institutions, for our collections, for our children. This book is for you and for them.

The Idea

Do we want our behavior to say to the public "we're wasteful and indifferent"?

—Ellie Altman, Director of the Adkins Arboretum, Maryland

ONCE WE were all good at environmental sustainability. As long as we had to find it or make it, haul it or dump it, we only used as much as we could handle or pay others to handle for us. Innovation, specialization, and consumer demand led us to a state of heavy consumption and waste. Hopefully innovation, specialization, and consumer demand can shift the balance.

We want you to be green because it supports your mission (every institution's—not just science museums), saves money (more than the myths will lead you to believe), and can make a positive impact on the environment while encouraging staff, board, volunteers, and visitors to do the same in their lives.

Green in museums is the best example of museums as community partners.

Green Is Good for All Museums

Not everyone is there yet, but many museums are thinking about how green fits into their vision, mission, and practices. The default position, for some, has been "sorry, green is not our mission." Many non-science or non-nature-related museums across the country tell us that environmental practice is not part of their mission. The art and history museums are the quickest to say so. That is simply not true and here is why: green can save you money that you can spend on carrying out core responsibilities, and green keeps the environment clean and safe for your objects, buildings, and visitors. Isn't that mission support?

Preservation is the mission for historic sites and for art, history, and natural history museums. Curators and collections managers know the weight of their charge to do no harm and preserve in perpetuity. They also know that preserving the past requires controlled climate conditions—the microclimate inside the museum and the macroclimate of the world's environment. The issues are the same whether we are discussing objects kept inside or buildings exposed to weather and airborne particulates from pollution. Environmentally insensitive building and operational practices contribute to degradation of the objects we are trying to save.

It is an "Aha!" moment when museum staff and board members realize the multiple connections between environmentally responsible practices and their institution's mission, their goals, and their future. Ronald L. Hurst, the Carlisle H. Humelsine Chief Curator and the Vice President of Collections and Museums at Colonial Williamsburg Foundation says that personally he "feels strongly about environmental sustainability" and "has guilt" over the energy consumption in museums. Under his watch, environmental sustainability has become an important operating principal in support of collections care. "It's exciting to find ways to care for collections and save energy."

Green makes sense and it is getting easier. Any second now your internal and external audiences will demand it of you. You should start right away if you want to have any chance of beating the curve. You may feel that green is a fad and you do not want chase a fad. Well, green is becoming mainstream because of its importance, not its fashion. With a little help from early adopters, packagers, and promoters, green value is moving the market. Our culture is changing and it is shaping our economy. The shortcut economy, the economy of excess and convenience, is giving way to a more sustainable economy. Don't we want to show our supporters and guests, who recognize this change, that we follow building and operational practices that contribute to preservation while also offering fascinating educational opportunities and saving money? Of course. Many institutions in the preservation business are making clear the dollar and environmental cost of collections care and are demonstrating solutions that are responsible and use resources wisely. These institutions are also mining educational opportunities as they explain their actions and encourage others to consider their own.

Surely the new green economy has and will continue to develop its own excesses and shortcuts, but the equation should come out more favorably for our environment and our world. The trick is to pay attention to true costs. Those who assume an added expense for green buildings are succumbing to myth and poor math. The math error is calculating only cost and ignoring direct and in-kind income. The income side of the budget includes direct and indirect cost savings, buy-backs, and life cycle costs. The myth problem is that green implementation often used to be more expensive than traditional methods. Today, the average cost of green building matches the average cost of traditional building.[1] For nearly all green building, the cost savings over time will more than balance the equation, and the positive consequences of reduced environmental impact will improve the balance.

But what if you are not building? What does it cost then? You control the math. You will choose some activities over others. Some will cost nothing; some will cost more; and some will cost less than what you are doing now. You can improve your energy efficiency (the greatest money saver over time) by upgrading and monitoring your systems and by changing some institutional habits. You can minimize your environmental impact by reducing waste, recycling, and sourcing green products and services. Not all the paybacks are as measurable as with reductions in energy and water use, but the cumulative value to the institution and to the planet is positive.

Synergy is where you will get your return on investment, whether you are calculating money, sustainability, or messaging. In fund-raising we preach that money must do more than one thing. You probably do this naturally: you apply for a grant that trains your staff in conservation principles to protect your collections and reduce outsourced conservation costs; or you are willing to purchase a particular plant collection management software because using the database provides more efficient record keeping and data backup opportunities and offers web access to well-presented information for your education staff and the public. It is really just efficiency with funding and staff resources. Apply that philosophy to your green decisions, too.

When choosing something not green, because you think green is more expensive, you are choosing to not spend money on an aspect of your institution. For how long have museums been willing to pay more for what we feel we need: for our collections, for the public, for our donors? We have been buying acid-free materials since we recognized the need. Many have built that great reception hall for fund-raising events and earned income opportunities. All can cost more than other options. It will not be long before green is comprehensively required by code—it already is to varying degrees in different parts of the country. Wouldn't it be better to be ahead of the curve? To demonstrate you are community leaders that use resources wisely? To show you are willing to invest in the future? That you are here for the long haul? When someone says to you "what does it cost to go green," you can look them right in the eye and say "what does it cost *not* to go green?"[2]

Need to Replace Your Boiler?

Use the opportunity to upgrade to an energy-efficient system and save money on your utilities. The change will probably give you a bit more space for storage or other utilities at the same time.

Rethinking Pavement on Your Site?

A bioswale (a biological water holding and filtering swale) can reduce your stormwater runoff (saving you money if you have to pay for sewer volume), reduce non-point source pollutants running into the water system, and add low-maintenance landscaping—particularly if you use native plant materials. If the bioswale replaces impervious surface, then you are also reducing heat island effect.

Want to Institutionalize Staff Recycling Efforts?

Recycling programs can earn income, reduce tipping fees, and increase public engagement.

So how exactly do we make these choices? Well, there are shades of green; some of us will be more green than others will be, personally and professionally. The environmental sustainability of your institution is a mission-based decision; implementation should come from mission-driven decisions made on a daily basis using your institutional policy for green.

If you have not yet developed policy, you should, but in the meantime ask yourself: "Does this green element build institutional capacity, directly or indirectly?" and "Does this green element increase our mission-related public value, directly or indirectly?" Increasing capacity improves our ability to fulfill our missions, and increasing our public value within our missions is our job anyway. So "yes" for either question means pursue the green solution. When it is yes for both, then all that is left to consider is how it fits with other components and how to phase it in.

Collections Care

Care and preservation of collections is energy and resource intensive and inextricably connected to the health of the global environment. Display lighting and climate maintenance, water, food, and habitat, housing, crating, and special transport all cost museums money and impact the environment. For institutions with living collections (or those nonliving collecting institutions that educate about the earth or space), their preservation mission is so clearly connected to environmental issues. The curators of these organizations are largely scientists who easily connect their conservation mission to sustainable practice. Many have designed low-impact field stations using vernacular materials and strategies. The Wildlife Conservation Society's Belize station was built in 1993. The structure has composting toilets and relies on wind and solar energy and sits lightly on a pristine atoll. Choosing green in that context is easy.

For institutions caring for nonliving collections, it has taken longer to connect the dots between environmental sustainability and the preservation of tools and ceramics, archives and highboys, paintings and textiles. Curators and collection managers take to heart the phrase "in perpetuity" for collections care. This charge has a global dimension since the planet is the ultimate housing for collections. Paying attention to mitigating global levels of pollution is an important aspect of mission fulfillment for those in the preservation business. Pollution in Los Angeles is made of toxic particulates from China—the very same particulates museums are trying to keep away from objects. The severity of floods and other natural disasters is widely seen as a product of global climate change, in turn a result of poor environmental practice. Since 2005, when Hurricanes Katrina and Rita destroyed or damaged a swath of our cultural heritage on the Gulf Coast, staff and policymakers at art and history museums as well as libraries and archives have made the connection and have stepped up ways to reduce their environmental impact. Think of it as the ultimate in preventive conservation.

The connection between collections care—living and nonliving—and green practices is reinforced when considering risk management. The 2005 Heritage Health Index Report surveyed collecting institutions (e.g., museums, historical societies, government archives, libraries, scientific organizations, and universities) about conservation and preservation practices but also security, budgets, emergency planning, and facilities.[3] The results were dismal and laid bare the loss of and threats to collections from poor environmental controls, improper storage, inadequate staffing and financing, and poor planning for floods and other emergencies. The report did not include energy or water shortages in its list of risks to be managed and prepared for, but imagine yourself in the shoes of collections managers at Zoo Atlanta when drought caused water shortages in 2007. The severe conditions forced a quick response to conserve water to ensure enough for collections care (that is, the survival of real bongos and alligators and flamingos, among other creatures). Fortunately the zoo had conducted an audit of its water consumption in 2005, so already had in place the beginnings of plans to reduce water use. Immediate reduction measures included repairing the leaks in the flamingo pool to eliminate water loss and instituting an old-fashioned technique: cleaning areas by sweeping debris instead of hosing it away. California's fall 2007 wildfires affected national and local register properties, the park systems, and collecting institutions and tore through fifteen National Register historic districts. In La Jolla, 95 percent of historic adobe properties were lost, including an 1865 structure considered the oldest existing stone building in Malibu. Climate experts, including contributors to the Intergovernmental Panel on Climate Change, a co-recipient of the 2007 Nobel Peace Prize, connect these wildfires and droughts to climate change and predict they will only get worse.[4] Instituting water and energy conservation and other green practices that mitigate climate change are, without a doubt, mission activities for collecting institutions of all kinds.

Curators and collections managers have been following green practices for decades in their storage areas with attention to good air quality (using low-volatile organic compound or VOC materials and smart ventilation strategies) and reusing housing materials. Conservators have begun to engage in new thinking about storage climate control, pointing the way to significant energy savings in collections care. Microenvironments (conditioning a room within a room for vulnerable objects) and segregating materials by type help create optimal conditions for longevity while reducing energy use. Efficiencies and more effective climates can be achieved by storing all metals together, for example, or all glass together, and so on. Challenges remain: objects being rotated onto the exhibit floor must undergo a transitional acclimatizing process; curators will need to loosen their grip on their collections as objects under their purview are separated among several storage areas; and the limits of financial and human resource capacities constrain most institutions from undertaking these changes anytime soon. As larger institutions increase digitization of collection images, the need to actually handle objects decreases. An image of course can never replace the sheer joy of seeing the real thing, but being able to manage, compare, catalog, and research using sortable databases and images is a boon to collections care and protection, and supports the future vision of storage vaults segregated by materials. Some institutions have already begun to develop state-of-the-art collections care facilities off-site. This trend has the bonus of freeing valuable real estate in the museum proper for exhibits, programs, and income-generating functions. It improves energy efficiency by enabling integrated design of HVAC systems and the building envelope specifically to maintain climate conditions.

Next to energy use (for lighting and climate control), crating and ship- ping are generally seen to be the greatest resource link for institutions car- ing for fine and decorative art and artifacts. Imagine a typical scenario for a medium to large loan exhibition: construction of a custom travel crate to house each one of perhaps hundreds of objects. The crate serves its purpose and after the one- to two-year tour the object goes back into its storage hous- ing and the travel crate goes to the landfill. Collections managers, registrars, and art handlers recognize the dollar and environmental cost of these prac- tices. Later we will share the story of one museum's attempt to get started on change.

Green Is Here to Stay

A confluence of factors has brought environmental sustainability to the fore- front of people's consciousness, and if you are reading this book you are part of this trend. The environmental consequences of unchecked consumption of energy and water are affecting us all. Increases in health problems such as asthma, diabetes, and obesity are being connected to poor air quality and mass food production and processing. The increasing severity of natural dis- asters (hurricanes, flooding, and wildfires) threatens our communities and our museums. In response, green interest and industry are growing at a rapid pace and the numbers are staggering. There is eco-chic (supermodels have eco-friendly foundations, and green is fashionable); websites for green resources are proliferating (TreeHugger.com; grist.org; ecogeek.org; greenop- tions.com; worldchanging.com are just a few of the growing list); and NBC recently featured "Green Week" by weaving environmental storylines throughout that week's programming. Discovery Channel is planning the first-ever twenty-four-hour TV network dedicated solely to green lifestyle programming with interactive tools and how-to resources. Corporations have recognized that sustainability can contribute to profitability and add to the brand.

Infrastructure, training, and research and development to support green practices is growing. The U.S. Green Building Council's (USGBC) green building rating system LEED (Leadership in Energy and Environmental Design) has been an influential force in the marketplace, and the numbers of LEED-certified buildings are growing rapidly. Greenbuild, the USGBC's national conference, is also growing. The 2007 conference in Chicago had 25,000 attendees (up from over 13,000 in 2006) and Bill Clinton was the keynote speaker.[5] Manufacturers are keeping pace with interest in green practices and the range of energy- and water-efficient systems, and the avail- ability of recycled and low-VOC materials has grown as their price goes down. Similarly, localvore movements are promoting healthy eating with fresh, locally sourced and organic foods grown sustainably, without the poor land management practices that contribute to flooding, pesticides that introduce toxins to groundwater and our food stream, or long-distance carbon dioxide-producing transportation. Wal-Mart, the largest retailer in the world, sells green products.

Clearly green is quickly becoming mainstream. Some say the tipping point in acceptance has already arrived.

How Do You Know What Green Is?

We need both science and philosophy to understand the range of opportunity in going green. There are degrees of green, and there are green wannabes. Learning to distinguish them is important. In this book we frequently use the term *green* to suggest or describe the array of environmentally thoughtful practice in museums. Green is today's generic term for environmentally better practice. Even though people often use *green* and *sustainable* interchangeably, there are proper definitions: *green* refers to products and behaviors that are environmentally benign (we think of it as the "do no harm" clause), while *sustainable* means practices that rely on renewable or reusable materials and processes that are green or environmentally benign (we think of that as "do no harm and keep the patient alive"). Renewable and reusable are critical for keeping the planet-patient alive.

Greenwashing (adapted from whitewashing) means exaggerating green properties, or arbitrarily selecting the green aspects and ignoring the non-green aspects. The promoter may not take care to research or explain the extent of green, or will simply gloss over the data to capture the marketing appeal of green. Watchdog groups have sprung up to keep track of, and expose, flagrant and exaggerated appropriation of green value for corporate gain.[6] We discuss sourcing in chapter 3, but just as savvy shoppers question "natural" products, beware green claims. When a museum, a trusted resource, highlights and describes its green practices, it is contributing to public perception of what is truly green.

Institutions, including museums, are beginning to consider the environment in their assessments of their bottom line, but that bottom line has expanded. Instead of just being a single bottom line of profit, it is now a triple bottom line (TBL) for people, planet, and profit. Your institution's TBL should be able to show positive effects for people, the environment, and your income. The Phipps Conservatory and Botanical Gardens (Phipps), California Academy of Sciences (The Academy) and Oregon Museum of Science and Industry (OMSI) use the TBL as a touchstone to measure and evaluate their green activities around reductions in carbon dioxide (CO_2) and waste emissions through thoughtful energy use, choice of materials and processes, and in programming. We will discuss metrics and evaluations later, but each institution can find formative and summative evaluation mechanisms, TBL or other methods, suitable for their culture, mission, and scale.

What Makes Buildings, Sites, and Operations Green?

Sustainable design has come a long way from the days of hippie teepees and fringe passive solar designs. Today's systems and materials that are energy efficient and create healthy environments (for objects and people) are very sophisticated, and can and should be integrated into your physical plant and operational practices for maximum return and minimal impact whether you are building, renovating, or improving daily operations.

Sharon Park, FAIA, of the National Park Service provides this description: "While sustainable design is still being defined by many, for architecture there are perhaps major principles:

Provide a healthy environment for the workplace: good ventilation—strive for at least six air changes per hour as opposed to the traditional four; use of natural lighting, appealing work spaces, circulation patterns that encourage pedestrian movement; elimination of chemicals, air particulates, formaldehyde fumes, solvents, volatile organic compounds.

Select building technologies and materials that are "green"—use materials that are biodegradable, recyclable, and made from renewable resources and that have been manufactured in a way that has not damaged the environment; select replacement materials that have a high percentage of recyclable content; select long-lasting and low-energy-use products, such as specialized lightbulbs; retain materials in place to the extent possible; consider thermal glazing that can be added to historic windows.

Consume less energy in the new systems in the building than market standards—reduce ambient lighting and increase task lighting; use sensors, timers, and motion detectors to control energy use to fixtures; consider low wattage features, individual or zoned controls; use the most efficient energy system or alternative energy sources available, such as photovoltaic cells; keep systems well maintained to work at peak efficiency; consider use of low wattage bulbs to reduce office lighting from 4 watts per square foot to less than 1 watt per square foot, which will have a direct impact on cooling requirements.

Have a recycling plan for waste and water—establish areas for collection of recyclable materials by type (paper, plastic, glass, vegetable matter); consider composting for gardening and grounds use; select materials based on the ability to recycle them later; use captured rainwater for irrigation; and consider options for use of gray water from noncontaminated sources in the building.[7]

Green operational practices range from your cleaning and procurement procedures to café and retail operations, and can even reach as far as your investment portfolio:

Consider the products that come to your site for operations—for permanent or temporary use. Their life cycle costs are important: where they came from; what materials were used and how they were extracted, adapted, and combined; how the materials affect the health of your workers and the environment; how the product gets packaged and shipped; and how you will use and reuse or dispose of it. Bulk purchases often reduce packaging and may reduce transportation frequency.

Think locally—the USGBC addresses this. "Materials containing recycled content expand markets for recycled materials, slow the consumption of raw materials and reduce the amount of waste disposed of in landfills. Use of local materials supports local economies while reducing transportation impacts."[8]

Reexamine your operations—everything from the annual fund mailing to workshop lunches; waste management for school groups to exhibit design; visitor traffic patterns to furniture selection for the chairs around the board table. Can each one be done using different steps or methods that are more energy efficient or ecologically sound? The Environmental Protection Agency's (EPA) three Rs are key here: reduce how much you use (of everything—energy, water, products, etc.); reuse as much as possible of what you must use; and recycle what you have finished using.

Create a policy on environmental sustainability. This is the policy document that guides all decision making for the institution. Your business, investment, building, collections, personnel, and operational policies will all be affected by this. Use it to create guidelines for responsible practice.

Get the Green Word Out

Talking about environmental choices is as important as demonstrating them. Develop programming for each of your green activities. Find ways to tap into the current eco-consciousness and increase public engagement. It can be simple: many of us have e-mail newsletters. Remind folks, as Phipps does, that it is a "tree-free" newsletter. Add an e-mail tag of "Consider the environment before printing e-mails or attachments," or "To save a tree, limit printing of e-mails and attachments." Or you can be more engaging. Create on-site or take-it-home programming or use your websites to provide information that encourages green practices at home and in school or the workplace. The Grand Rapids Art Museum (GRAM) opened its new green building with an exhibition featuring the building's sustainable strategies and materials and their applications in international contexts (figure 1.1). The exhibition will get the green word out as it travels for a two-year run to art and design schools.

FIGURE 1.1. Tell your green story. Many aspects of sustainable design and environmentally responsible operational practices are not readily clear to visitors. Through education and explication, your audience can begin to connect the dots between conservation and preservation missions and global environmental health. The Grand Rapids Art Museum opened their new green building with an exhibition focusing on key elements of green design and the ways they are expressed in the building. In the exhibition, visitors learn about the LEED certification process and the importance of protecting the environment through innovative design and construction. © Image courtesy of Grand Rapids Art Museum and wHY Architecture

GRAND RAPIDS ART MUSEUM
Art and the Environment: Design Solutions

Natural light + energy saving features:
Resourceful use of natural light through large windows and skylights without harming the art.
3 layers of filters: exterior louvers, energy-saving insulated glass with argon gas and fabric scrim for light filtering in public area.

Green Housekeeping and strict recycling program.

Eco-friendly entrance
Large front portico (140 feet wide 120 feet deep) gives protection in the harsh winter and shade in the summer all year round.

Small building footprint
Leaving plans of the land for park, courtyards and water features.

Natural water recycling
Rain and snow water is stored and recycled for toilets, plant irrigation, pool and water features.

Energy-saving construction
Efficient insulation for solid concrete walls and glass walls.

Energy-saving skylights tailored to light levels for art
Natural light enters through triple-layered glass with ultraviolet protection and adjustable louvers to provide suitable light for the art.

Safe and energy-efficient indoor air quality control
Carbon dioxide monitoring, low-emitting materials and strict chemical / pollutant control.

Certified Wood Flooring
White oak planks used in the gallery come from sustainably harvested forests in the Northwest certified by Forest Stewardship Council.

Local Materials
Much of the building's materials are sourced locally – the concrete is made from cement, sand and stone from sources near Lake Michigan.

Use of recycled and recyclable materials
Building's insulation material made from recycled paper and fiber. Recyclable carpeting made from digestible corn-based plastic.

Public transportation friendly
Bicycle racks and staff showers in the facility.

Waste efficient landscape design.

Educate and inform this public about green building and the environment.

Regeneration of underdeveloped urban site.

Innovative Air-conditioning system
Energy-saving air conditioning uses 3 of 12-feet diameter energy wheels to bring indirect evaporative cooling method for air-conditioning. Ozone depletion policy.

copyrights of wHY Architecture, Los Angeles

The Cincinnati Zoo and Arboretum uses its website to educate about plant conservation issues, with articles on sustainable gardening and data on propagation, preservation, and restoration of endangered flora (e.g., one in every eight species of plant in the world is threatened with extinction). Zoo Atlanta's website has a conservation page with information about the Zoo's Green Team as well as a Green Tips section with information and resources for applying green measures at home and work. Many zoo websites offer information on environmental practices and connect it to their mission. For example, did you know about cell phones and the threat to gorillas? Zoos are making the connection for visitors between e-waste recycling and preservation of habitat for gorillas: coltan is a key ingredient of many electronics; it is mined primarily in the Democratic Republic of the Congo, right in the middle of gorilla habitat; mining has disrupted habitat and led to poaching of gorillas. Can you picture your public's response? Interpretation is our best opportunity for education and engagement.

Green Influence, Advocacy, and Market Muscle

As environmental sustainability becomes mainstream, many museums are finding they have an expanded role in educating about environmental issues and connecting them to their institutional missions. Showing visitors the consequences of overconsumption and poor environmental practices while also showing them alternatives to those behaviors is a way to stimulate collective action. Advocacy has been a touchy word in the museum community and many have adopted a "just-the-facts" approach, described by one science museum staff member this way: "We don't tell people not to smoke. We show them what smoking does, give the facts about the consequences of smoking." Many museums, because of their mission, situation, and capacity, choose to provoke thought and exploration to create understanding. Some, based on those same factors, will choose to provoke thought and exploration and encourage action. This engages the public and attracts visitation and support. Whether museums take the next step to advocacy is up to each, but the public currency of environmental sustainability is no longer a debate.

On the shores of Lake Champlain in Burlington, Vermont, stands ECHO Lake Aquarium and Science Center at the Leahy Center for Lake Champlain, the first LEED-certified building in Vermont. For ECHO staff it is important to change the way visitors look at the environment and make decisions. When considering fishing, lawn fertilizer, or anything else connected to the environment, executive director Phelan Fretz says, "We want to help people make . . . decisions by providing information. We're not an advocate for a particular position. We're an advocate for people having good information, and we're an advocate for good science." In San Francisco's Golden Gate Park, the California Academy of Sciences' (CAS's) new green facility is under development. Gregory C. Farrington, PhD, CAS executive director, describes their approach this way:

> We can serve as an honest broker in the debates that will have to occur around the choices society faces regarding sustainability. We can help provide education about the science surrounding these issues. We can spotlight important areas where further investigation is needed. But make no mistake: The California Academy stands for the central importance of scientific investigation and the scientific process in resolving critical questions.[9]

Either way, each museum is educating by example through their green building and operational practices.

Advocacy can take the form of educating about behavior change. Visitors to Chicago's Field Museum can pay an extra dollar for admission to offset the carbon emissions they generated in getting there. In the program's first three hours, 100 out of 549 visitors offset their emissions. Out of that 100, nine people paid more than one dollar. "Global warming is one of the most important issues today," said Kirk Anne Taylor, the Field Museum's urban conservation manager. "One of our missions is to engage the public in these issues, and this is a way to get people involved in reducing the impact they have on the environment."

In the Pacific Northwest, the Bonneville Environmental Foundation supports watershed restoration and renewable energy projects. It also sells what are called green tags:

> carbon offsets as renewable energy certificates … to replace traditional polluting sources of electricity with clean, secure, and sustainable renewable sources of energy that come from solar and wind power from across North America.[10]

Any individual or organization can buy tags. You could offer or require tag purchasing as part of the rental price of your facilities.

In St. Michaels, Maryland, the Chesapeake Bay Maritime Museum (CBMM) interprets and preserves the culture of the region, a culture once based almost entirely on the Chesapeake Bay, the largest estuary in the United States. The open-air museum on eighteen acres at the water's edge is a very popular destination (figure 1.2). Still, president Stuart Parnes is concerned. He says, "I've been asked, if the museum prospers while the Bay dies, 'What's the

FIGURE 1.2. Campus greening. Self-assessment and planning is important in any greening process; it is critical when you are dealing with an entire campus. The Chesapeake Bay Maritime Museum in St. Michaels, Maryland, began its process by hosting a free workshop exploring campus greening for area nonprofits, then moved to an overview of its own existing practices before beginning its green team effort. Courtesy of Aloft Aerial Photography

point?'" The museum's mission is to preserve the culture of this region, he says, "but we all recognize that this means more than collecting physical artifacts. If we are going to preserve the very tenuous culture of the Bay's people, we need to help sustain the Bay." Now, through greening the museum campus, and expanding environmental programming, the museum is choosing to add environmental sustainability to its repertoire. CBMM will add sustainability interpretation on-site and in the community in concert with converting to a sustainable campus and marina. "Everything we do here is because of, and about, the Bay," says director of education Robert Forloney. "We haven't taken on the challenge of sustaining the Bay, yet everything—vessel design, culture and lifeways, and folk traditions—is based on the Bay." He talks about how the museum can help the public understand the complexities of the situation, how we got to this state, remind us all of the cultural and natural heritage of the area, and be more active in the discussion. The museum can be a moderator for opposing views, a center for discussion, and a leader by example.[11]

The mission of the Monterey Bay Aquarium (MBAq) is to inspire the conservation of the oceans. Its mantra is "inspire, engage and empower," so every program includes those three components: inspire visitors by showing them live animals; engage the visitor by making connections between themselves and the animal world; and empower visitors with opportunities to make a difference. Playful and lovable sea otters are a very important part of the MBAq experience. The popular sea otter exhibit and Take Action web page explain that coastal pollution may be limiting the rate of recovery for the wild sea otter population, and part of the problem is parasites, one being *Toxoplasma gandii.* Many of us are familiar with the warning to pregnant women not to handle cat litter from their pets. The parasite in cat feces that affects pregnant humans affects sea otters too. Cat litter flushed down the toilet gives parasites a pathway to the ocean. After a visit to MBAq, the young son of a California legislator told his dad, "We've got to do something. The otters are dying." His father took that message to work and in September 2006 it became law that cat litter sold in California must carry warning labels against flushing soiled litter or dumping it in storm sewers. The law raised maximum fines for harassing sea otters in state waters to $25,000 with an equal fine for harassment in federal waters. The legislation also introduced on the California state income tax form a new provision to enable taxpayers to contribute to the aquarium's Sea Otter Research Fund. All residents of California are now connected, through their tax forms, to the issue and to the aquarium's conservation mission.

Sometimes museums directly influence businesses and corporations to consider instituting green practices. The Monterey Bay Aquarium's Seafood Watch program has helped a major supermarket make changes to sustainable seafood efforts, and worked with a large food vendor to make and promote its commitment to sustainable food sourcing for the company's 400-plus institutional café clients. In Peoria, Illinois, green principles informed plans for a seven-and-a-half-acre downtown building and site development for the Peoria Riverfront Museum (a collaborative effort of seven organizations). Museum Square is a planned mixed-use development that also includes a visitor center for Caterpillar, the world's leading manufacturer of construction and mining equipment, diesel and natural gas engines, and industrial gas turbines. According to Jim Richerson, president and CEO of Lakeview Museum of Arts and Sciences, the lead organization in this public-private partnership, the museum's interest in LEED inspired Caterpillar to pursue LEED in the building of their visitor center. It would be the corporation's first LEED-certified building. Caterpillar's first corporate sustainability report was in 2005. Its nearly 60,000-square-foot building planned as part of the downtown Museum Square project was registered for LEED-NC in November 2005.[12]

In Boston, at the Museum of Fine Arts, staff were preparing for construction to begin on a major expansion and renovation. The task for Matthew Siegal, head of the Conservation and Collections Management Department, was to plan the packing and transport of 85,000 chairs and tall clocks, porcelain and textiles, and all manner of other objects to an off-site storage facility where they would remain for several years while demolition, construction, and fit-out of the new American Wing took place. Remember the discussion about waste in collections care in the crating and shipping of objects? Well, Siegal and his staff figured there had to be a better way. To eliminate the duplication of effort and resources in designing and building travel crates and then in turn designing and building longer-term housing for the objects, the team devised a generic system that can be customized to accommodate a wide range of objects, including delicate gilded or painted surfaces or delicate upholstery (operative word...delicate). Conservators and collections managers worked hand-in-hand with major international art handling companies on the move. These same companies learned from the experience and have now in turn adopted these crate and housing specifications for their businesses. Museums making a difference.

There are major efforts across the country to make conferences and conventions green, and the museum industry is part of this effort. For the last several years the American Association of Museums' (AAM) conference has seen an increase in the number of sessions with green topics, and a fair number of conference goers have asked for a greener conference, including reductions in paper and product giveaways.[13] AAM has created a webpage called Greensteps to identify the steps it is taking to lessen its impact. The Mid-Atlantic Association of Museums will be greening its next conference, too. The Associations of Zoos and Aquariums (AZA) has been ramping up their green conference efforts, first in Tampa in 2006 and to a greater extent in 2007 in Philadelphia. The Association of Science and Technology Centers (ASTC) has also begun greening efforts. The National Association of Interpreters (NAI) noted the environmental impacts associated with bringing large numbers of people to a conference site and has made a commitment to green their annual national workshop with paperless communications, locally sourced food, hotels that donate leftover food to food banks, green hotel practices, on-site recycling, and leaving a positive environmental legacy with a local organization. The California Association of Museums (CAM) has a Green Museums Initiative to inspire California museums to develop green business practices, eco-friendly facility management, and sustainable programming. As part of this effort they have greened their annual conference with:

> 100 percent organic cotton tote bags;
> Conference program printed with vegetable ink on recycled paper;
> Sustainable cuisine whenever possible;
> Use of real tableware and linens at meals;
> Corn plastic plates and recycled paper napkins at some evening events;
> Created a carbon neutral event by offsetting conference greenhouse gas emissions;

Flyers printed on 100 percent postconsumer waste paper with vegetable
inks;

Printing eco-audit; and

Recycling at events.

A quick perusal of conference programs for these industry associations shows
a steady and marked increase in sessions dealing with environmental sustainability. At AAM in Boston in 2006 there was one session. At AAM Chicago in
2007 there were over ten sessions dealing with the topic. These associations
are also accepting grassroots formations of green committees. AZA has had
for years a Green Practices Scientific Advisory Group (SAG). The group's listserve is a well-used forum for sharing ideas and green practices and answer-
ing questions. Long-time chair of the group, Dr. Christine Sheppard, curator
of ornithology at the Wildlife Conservation Society's Bronx Zoo, says: "We
started the listserve in 2002 and since then it has grown to include over 550
members from all areas: AZA folks, green team coordinators, education people, NGO and government people. Green practices are an obvious fit for the
museum community and we can learn a lot from one another." The Green
Practices SAG will soon have an expanded presence on AZA's website. The
page will include a Frequently Asked Questions (FAQ) section that will cover
everything from tips on energy conservation (e.g., turn out the lights) to environmental impact comparisons between cloth and disposable diapers. Sheppard's latest campaign is getting the word out about "bird stripes" on
windows. She said billions of birds are killed annually by flying into glass on
buildings. Mitigating measures are easy to do and can save many birds. This
information and more is shared through the Green Practices SAG.[14]

AAM and the American Public Gardens Association accepted green
professional interest groups in 2007. The mission statement of AAM's Professional Interest Committee on Green Museums is "to support green
museum initiatives through dialogue, sharing data and case studies, and
networking that leads to professional development and environmentally
sustainable innovations." In 1999, before the public was talking about climate change, the New England Science Center Collaborative (NESCC)
raised a significant green flag. NESCC recognized that a wealth of climate
change research was going on in leading universities and it was unknown
to the public. The media was focused on climate change as a controversial
issue. To raise the level of scientific discourse, NESCC focused on working
with regional museums, planetariums, and aquariums to identify ways to
disseminate the research. After five years and many successful programs,
the sixty-member organization requested NESCC move from climate
change literacy into solutions programs. The result was the NESCC Green-

ing Our Science Centers Initiative. This hands-on program offers technical assistance, facility assessments, and peer networking to help informal educators at science museums jump start or further integrate green policies and activities into the operation of their organizations. Around the country there are various technical assistance, training, and advocacy programs helping institutions, including museums, go green: The GreenRountable, Rocky Mountain Institute, the Natural Step Network, and NESCC's parent organization, Clean Air–Cool Planet.

Environmental issues among museums are global. ASTC is made up of more than 540 members in forty countries. Their IGLO (International Action on Global Warming) Initiative raises worldwide public awareness about global warming and how the polar regions profoundly influence the earth's climate, environments, ecosystems, and human society. The IGLO website offers a toolkit of educational tools for educating about climate change and the importance of the polar regions. The National Trust in the UK has very clearly articulated policies around environmentally sustainable practices and in 2005 the Centre for Sustainable Heritage produced a groundbreaking study as a call for action.[15] Museums Australia, the national museum association of Australia, has a museums and sustainability policy to guide and support its membership around responsible practices.[16] Globally, green is part of the field's future.

Synergies with Existing Green Practices

Across the world governmental policies around energy and water use are driving both public and private developments. To underscore the global nature of the climate change problem and consolidate effort, international groups have sprung up. The International Council for Local Environmental Initiatives (ICLEI), with membership of 700 local governments representing over 300 million people worldwide, and initiatives like Cities for Climate Protection aim to reduce greenhouse gas emissions, improve air quality, and enhance urban sustainability. To reduce greenhouse gas emissions and realize multiple benefits for their communities, many U.S. cities have mandated sustainable design policies and, at the municipal, state, and regional levels, there are complicated policies and agreements around water use and access.

On the federal level, sustainable design has been incorporated into projects. Starting in the late 1990s, executive orders addressed waste reduction and water use. In 1999 Executive Order 13123, Greening the Government through Efficient Energy Management, required the Department of Defense, the General Services Administration, and the Department of Energy to provide sustainable design training to their staff. In January 2007 an executive order called upon all federal agencies to reduce energy intensity, or consumption per square foot, by 30 percent. The order also called for increases in the percentage of renewable sources in each agency's energy supply, and asked agencies to implement renewable energy generation projects on their property. Did you know that the White House has solar panels on its roof?

In 1995 the National Park Service (NPS) held its first sustainability charrette at Virgin Islands National Park. The result was an energized sustainability movement within the NPS and guidelines followed for incorporating sustainable design into NPS building and construction projects. Following a 2002 partnership with the EPA, the NPS embarked on more proactive outreach and education. It held greening charrettes at ten parks across the country for staff, other organizations, neighbors, and partners to share information and assist in specific greening efforts. Each park in turn developed goals around environmental leadership and planning, transportation, facilities, operations and maintenance, interpretation and education, and procurement. The NPS-EPA partnership has been branded as the Climate Friendly Parks Program with outcomes as diverse as Yosemite National Park's free shuttle service on hybrid buses and waste stream management at Glacier National Park. At Yosemite the program is not only saving money with fuel efficiency and reducing the environmental impact of over 3 million annual visitors, but the quality of the experience has improved with reduced traffic, noise, and exhaust smells. Green procurement, sustainability education, concessions environmental management, and incorporation of environmental management into project management are strategies covered in the Climate Friendly Parks workshops. Staff and partners acquire the tools to develop policies specific to their park's circumstances and opportunities. For example, at the Statue of Liberty and Ellis Island the concessionaire now recycles 75 percent of the waste generated by its own operations, by park visitors, and by the ferry concessioner that serves the islands—more than 350,000 pounds of trash a year.

Spectacularly beautiful, Zion National Park in Utah is a leader and model for sustainable operations and building practices among the parks in the national system. It was on the verge of being loved to death—park visitation doubled between 1982 and 1997—when park staff began working with the local community to address the sheer volume of cars and buses in the area. The park's 1996 Comprehensive Plan addressed sustainable design for transportation and buildings. In 2000 the Zion Visitor's Center, a soup-to-nuts model for sustainable design strategies, opened and the greening of the park has continued to be integrated into all areas of operations, design, policy, management, and interpretation.

It goes without saying that the idea of environmentally sustainable practices has particular meaning for NPS scientists, researchers, and staff on the front lines of climate change. They monitor dramatic changes to glaciers, measure profound impacts on hydrology and ecology, and see threats to the natural and cultural resources we are entrusted to preserve and protect. Solutions require collective action. Leigh Welling, director of Crown of the Continent Research Learning Center, Glacier National Park, points out:

> In the last several years I have witnessed a distinct shift in people's awareness that suggests we may be entering a solution-finding phase on climate change. We are moving into a new paradigm for problem-solving which is based on the assumption that everyone can contribute something of value. This is a learning community approach where we all participate as both teachers and learners. Through this technique, innovative and sustainable lifestyle and management strategies can emerge that maintain and improve environmental health as well as our quality of life.[17]

The building design and construction industry has taken up this challenge. The USGBC is a nonprofit organization that was founded in 1993 by a group of architects, engineers, and construction experts to transform the way buildings are designed, built, and operated. The council is membership based and consensus driven and now includes over 10,000 member companies and organizations and a network of more than seventy local chapters, affiliates, and organizing groups. The LEED rating system was introduced in 2000 to provide a technically rigorous system for ranking levels of greenness and has become an established brand and market force. In addition, architects have laid down a gauntlet and challenged the industry to dramatically and immediately reduce the building sector's carbon emissions with a goal of new buildings to be carbon neutral by the year 2030. The 2030 Challenge has been adopted by the U.S. Conference of Mayors, the American Institute of Architects, USGBC, National Association of Counties, and numerous states, counties, and cities.

Clearly, with the urgency around addressing climate change and solutions devised from so many sectors, there is a great deal of synergy to be had for museums that participate in finding solutions and helping spread the word. In Chicago, synergy both between museums and municipal government and among Chicago museums proper led to a green museum consortium. The Green Museums Steering Committee was founded in 2005. It receives support from the city's Department of the Environment. Working together to promote green museum operations, exhibits, and programming, the member organizations include:

John G. Shedd Aquarium
Peggy Notebaert Nature Museum
Adler Planetarium
Art Institute of Chicago/School of the Art Institute of Chicago
Museum of Contemporary Art
Museum of Science and Industry
The Field Museum

There are four subcommittees:

Green Museums Awards Subcommittee is responsible for establishing a certification program whereby member institutions annually demonstrate progress toward program goals.

The Knowledge Transfer Subcommittee is responsible for sharing best practices among member institutions.

The Joint Green Procurement Subcommittee examines and makes recommendations on pooled purchasing opportunities among member institutions.

The Programming and Outreach Subcommittee examines ways in which the Steering Committee can promote environmental awareness in the community.

In Portland, on the shores of the Willamette River, sits the Oregon Museum of Science and Industry. The complex occupies a former brownfield. In 1990, during a period of the museum's redevelopment, there were no city or state regulatory design requirements for stormwater discharges into the river. Seeing an opportunity to test new strategies, the city asked OMSI to rework its parking lot design to introduce bioswales. These landscaped areas capture water runoff, retaining and cleansing it of silt and pollution before it is released into the watershed or storm sewer. The new design filtered the runoff from four acres of parking lots and prevented more than 3.9 million gallons of untreated stormwater runoff from discharging directly into the Willamette River annually. OMSI's project schedule was not disrupted, and the museum saved $78,000 in construction because it eliminated the need for stormwater pipes, sedimentation manholes, and catch basins. OMSI's collaborative approach to site design led to important revisions in Portland's municipal codes governing stormwater management and parking lots. The new codes in turn protect the river.[18] OMSI is now collaborating with Oregon Health and Science University around infrastructure issues as OHSU develops a new campus in OMSI's South Waterfront District. As OMSI considers its next phase of development, they are hoping to learn lessons from OHSU on developing a carbon neutral campus. OHSU's first building in the new development, the sixteen-story, 400,000-square-foot Center for Health and Healing, has achieved LEED Platinum rating—the highest available.

The common educational mission of museums and colleges and universities is fertile ground for partnerships and collaborations. Colleges began to green their campuses almost twenty years ago. A 1990 declaration from a group of university leaders acknowledged that universities have a major role in addressing environmental changes. Oberlin College was one of the first ten signatories to the American College and University Presidents Climate Commitment and has been cited for its innovative approaches to sustainability on campus, including food service, in which 30 percent of what is served is sourced locally. The Allen Memorial Art Museum on campus has 12,000 works of art that provide a comprehensive overview of the history of art. The planned renovations to its buildings (1917, 1977) include a LEED Silver goal in line with university policy. Bowdoin College Art Museum just completed a renovation and expansion that includes geothermal wells for heating and cooling. In summer 2007 Bowdoin signed the Climate Commitment and its president has pledged to move toward a carbon neutral campus.

The American College and University Presidents Climate Commitment is in many ways an outgrowth of the Talloires Declaration, a document signed in 1990 that recognized higher education institutions have a role to play in solving environmental issues. It was a watershed moment that galvanized and accelerated fledgling campus sustainability efforts that had sprouted up during the 1970s energy crisis.[19] Grassroots clamoring by students and staff for attention to the environmental impact of campuses is now driving university policy on energy, water use, recycling, and waste reduction. As a result of overarching policies, university museums are also pursuing green practices. Many are leading the charge by being the first sites on campus to go green.

At the University of Oklahoma, the Sam Noble Oklahoma Museum of Natural History is one of the largest academically based natural history museums in the world, with more than 7 million objects and a mission to inspire people to understand the natural and cultural world through collection-based discovery, interpretation, and education. The museum has registered its seven-year-old, 195,000-square-foot building for LEED for Existing Buildings (LEED-EB) certification. The USGBC initiated LEED-EB in 2005 to evaluate maximum operating efficiency and minimal environmental impact in existing buildings. The museum's goal is to be the first LEED building on the 24,000-student campus, and the first existing building in Oklahoma to become LEED-certified. Director Ellen Censky says she feels it is important that the museum have a bully pulpit from which it can promote environmental awareness—throughout the museum industry, Oklahoma, and her community. "It is part of our mission and vision to inspire understanding, appreciation and stewardship of the earth and its peoples," she says. "If we cannot lead by example, then why should people listen to what we are saying?"[20]

For-profit developers are also building green. In a sector known for keeping a keen eye on the bottom line, the rise in new green residential and commercial office construction is another signifier of the green tipping point for profitability and marketability. The cost of green design and construction has decreased as the skills and materials marketplace has responded to the need and interest. Do not underestimate the marketing cachet of green. The National Building Museum's exhibit The Green House: New Directions in Sustainable Architecture and Design created such a demand from new volunteers that the museum offered a second training session for docents, and at one point attendance at the museum had risen 46 percent during the exhibit. It was stunningly popular. The show has been packaged and is traveling, and the exhibition's collateral materials are still available on the museum's webpage. The museum is continuing the green exhibition series with Green Communities in 2009.

The connections between good practice, good business, and good publicity have been made by the nation's largest theme park operators: the Walt Disney Company, Busch Entertainment Corporation, and Universal Studios. Disney has branded their green awareness with the term "environmentality," has created two top-level environmental corporate positions and is addressing waste, energy use, and toxic chemical use throughout its hotels and parks. The need to comprehensively address their environmental practices may have been underscored for Disney by the Center for Health, Environment and Justice. In April 2007, the center launched the Disney Go Green Campaign to urge Disney to use certified green cleaning products and practices. The center noted that Disney avoids the use of toxic cleaning chemicals at Animal Kingdom to protect animals; however, toxic products were used around children in their many parks, hotels, and restaurants. Meanwhile, Universal Orlando pledged to leave what President Bill Davis called the "smallest environmental-impact footprint possible." This initiative is part of the Green is Universal campaign by corporate parents NBC Universal and General Electric Co. Busch Entertainment Corporation's nine parks entertain more than 20 million guests a year and employ more than 15,000 people. At SeaWorld, Busch Gardens, and Discovery Cove staff steward the largest animal collection in the world, so it is not surprising that Busch has been supporting wildlife conservation through funded research and education and has made efforts at recycling and other environmental practices at the parks.

What is relatively new is environmentalism's role in the corporate hierarchies and the resulting integrated approaches to sustainable practices. Again, we should not be surprised. According to an online survey by the travel Website Orbitz, over two-thirds (67 percent) of Americans place importance on the eco-friendliness of a destination.[21] The opportunities to learn from others and to exert market muscle through consortia and partnerships are especially ripe in the community of for-profit and nonprofit stewards of living collections. Such elevation of sustainability standards is good for the industry and will "raise all boats in the water," as John Linehan, president and CEO of Zoo New England, put it, saying, "That's the thing with this group. We don't mind everyone copying each other and sharing knowledge since we are all committed to conservation."

Turning the Idea into Policy and Public Trust

Each of the institutions in this book is in a different stage of implementing sustainable practices. Few have policies on environmental sustainability, but most realize policy is critical for success. Colleges, universities, and many corporations are far ahead of museums in this effort. We believe that policies on environmental sustainability will soon become a professional expectation for all types of organizations, not just museums.

Policy institutionalizes behavior by providing vision and frameworks, defining process, identifying goals and evaluation methods, and delegating authority. You may create a policy that stands alone, or one that is woven into existing policies. What matters is that it provides a responsive framework for decision making. CBMM is learning about sustainable behavior and policy, and is drafting policy. Colonial Williamsburg Foundation has an expectation of sustainable behavior across the organization; so far it has been applied on a case-by-case basis, but eventually it will work its way into policy. MBAq has had a policy on environmentally sensitive business practices for nearly a decade. It is very sophisticated and far-reaching and we have reproduced it here in its entirety as an important resource. Policies at OMSI and Madison Children's Museum (MCM) are good examples to start with, too.

Policy Components

GUIDING PRINCIPLE The environmental sustainability of your institution is a mission-based decision; implementation should come from mission-driven decisions on a daily basis. So what is your mission-related position on sustainability? MCM has what it calls sustainability commitment: "We focus on children, including their future. We are committed to being a sustainable organization, balancing economic, social, and environmental factors to help ensure that we meet our present needs, while enabling future generations to meet their needs. We empower and equip children to actively shape the world they will inherit." Here is an adaptation of an idea from Piacentini at the Phipps: We are going to operate [the museum] like we care about [the Bay/the Susquehanna River Watershed/the long-term protection of world heritage/species diversity].

PURPOSE: WHY AND WHAT OMSI says that it "has adopted sustainability as a strategic value" and that it "tries to make its decisions based upon the triple bottom line of environmental, social, and fiscal responsibility." It focuses its sustainability efforts in four areas—large ones, but clearly identified areas—CO_2 emission reduction, waste reduction and prevention, exhibit production, and public education.[22] MCM also defines four focus areas, but with a more generalized format:

As educational and community leaders, we will:

Integrate the principles of sustainability into all major business decisions
Seek strategic collaborations
Evaluate and reduce the environmental impacts of our operations
Design and develop our products, services, and materials with the
long-term health of our children and community in mind[23]

AUTHORITY, COMMITMENT, AND OVERSIGHT: WHO, HOW, AND SO ON Policy development and implementation require full participation by the board and staff leadership, with understanding of all staff ramifications. Developing this policy is not a one-person job; it is an institution's job—or it must be if it is going to work. OMSI's committee has a chair from senior management, and departmental participation from exhibits, programs, finance, human resources, maintenance, and sponsorship. Among other charges, its role is to:

Serve as a central point of information and communication on issues
and projects related to sustainability
Identify projects that move us closer to performance targets and meet
triple-bottom-line standards of success
Prioritize and intensify activities throughout the organization
Document and communicate progress within this area

Action plans implement policy. Your green team's action plan will be a significant part of the institution's sustainability action plan. This is where you should identify evaluation methods and goals. OMSI's work plan for fiscal year 2008 had these actions steps:

Propose for adoption performance targets for the organization's sustainability efforts

Identify, research, and prioritize areas of greatest potential impact related to sustainability

Advise senior management of these opportunities and propose a plan to address them

Serve as a resource to accomplish projects approved by senior management

Drive internal communication of progress and success

Serve as a resource for emergent and cutting-edge sustainability issues

Public Expectations

Some of the larger institutions with sustainable public messages have attracted public scrutiny for their endowment portfolio holdings in companies associated with highly unsustainable business practices. Disney attracted the attention of a group dedicated to promoting human health and environmental integrity (the operative word is *integrity*) and now is addressing sustainability from the top tier of the corporate structure.

Museums can take heed of that message and be wary of jumping in too fast and branding themselves as environmental leaders without demonstrating sustainability throughout the organization, both in front of the house (where visitors can see the recycling in their food service operation), and in back of the house (is your dumpster filled with landfill-bound materials that could be recycled?). "Walking the talk" is an oft-cited phrase to describe people who practice what they preach. If museums are to reap the full benefits of going green, and that includes public trust, developing comprehensive policy that covers all aspects of their business is the best route to success on all levels.

As you raise your green flag you may be asked some tough questions. Is your mission to conserve marine life yet your endowment is based on profits from corporations whose practices are harming the animals you are trying to save? Are staff housed in moldy, cramped quarters with poor air quality, as is the case with one prominent environmental organization? Making a commitment to environmental responsibility, making your plan known and transparent, while indicating it is a complicated journey that requires funding, can only do you good and will rally those in a position to help you.

Policies on environmental sustainability are not yet common in the field, but there are some in existence. Every institution will obviously have a different configuration according to their scale, mission, and circumstance, but we want to reinforce the importance of buy-in on a policy from every corner of the organization from the board through all staff levels and volunteers, with public support.

This brings us back to the core question Ellie Altman asked: "Do we want our behavior to say to the public 'we're wasteful and indifferent'?" Do you want to say that? Or would you rather your behavior said "We are resourceful and engaged!"

Notes

1. Lisa Fay Matthiessen and Peter Morris, "The Cost of Green Revisited: Reexamining the Feasibility and Cost Impact of Sustainable Design in the Light of Increased Market Adoption," www.davislangdon.com/USA/Research/ResearchFinder/2007-The-Cost-of-Green-Revisited/, accessed August 1, 2007.

2. Barbara Batshalom of the Green Roundtable introduced this concept at the New Hampshire AIA Integrated Design Integrated Development 2006 conference. We have been using it ever since to draw attention to the need to look at savings on future energy costs as a measurement of value.

3. *A Public Trust at Risk: The Heritage Health Index Report on the State of America's Collections*, HHI Heritage Health Index, a partnership between Heritage Preservation and the Institute of Museum and Library Services, 2005. www.heritagepreservation.org/hhi/, accessed December 19, 2007.

4. Oregon State University, "Massive California Fires Consistent with Climate Change, Experts Say," *ScienceDaily*, October 24, 2007. www.sciencedaily.com/releases/2007/10/071024103856.htm, accessed December 4, 2007.

5. According to the Greenbuild website, the annual conference is a two-time IMEX Environmental Meeting Award recipient, and the organization strives to leave a legacy of improved environmental practices in each of the host cities. For example, Greenbuild Denver implemented the first recycling program in the Colorado Convention Center, which the CCC continued even after the conference left. More than 100 percent of the emissions associated with Greenbuild are offset via Cleaner and Greener certification. USGBC also works with Meeting Strategies Worldwide to implement a number of green strategies at each of the conferences.

6. Groups like CorpWatch, GreenBiz, and Co-op America are regular critics of greenwashing.

7. Sharon C. Park, "Sustainable Design and Historic Preservation," *Cultural Resource Management*, No. 2, National Park Service, 1998.

8. United States Green Building Council, *Existing Buildings, version 2.0, Reference Guide* 2nd ed. Washington, DC: USGBC, 2006, p. 251.

9. www.calacademy.org/newacademy/academy/building/our_green_practices.php, accessed November 18, 2007.

10. www.greentagsusa.org/GreenTags/index.cfm, accessed December 19, 2007.

11. Sarah S. Brophy and Elizabeth Wylie, adapted material first appeared in "The Greener Good: The Enviro-Active Museum," *Museum News*, January–February 2008.

12. Jim Richerson, "Creating the Green Museum: Making Museums Matter for Community Sustainability," paper presented at annual meeting of the American Association of Museums, Chicago, May 2007. As of this writing, funding for the Museum Square complex is uncertain.

13. Our own green session evaluations have consistently included expressions of this sort and the large conference "comment wall" has also shown an increase in wishes for a green conference.

14. www.aza.org/RC/RC_Green/.

15. M. Cassar, *Climate Change and the Historic Environment*, research report, Centre for Sustainable Heritage, University College London, 2005.

16. www.museumsaustralia.org.au/dbdoc/sustainability.pdf, accessed December 12, 2007.

17. Leigh Welling, "Forum: Climate Change—From Knowledge to Action," *Sustainability News*, National Park Service, Fall 2006.

18. Brophy and Wylie, adapted from "Greener Good."

19. Peggy F. Barlett and Geoffrey W. Chase, eds., *Sustainability on Campus: Stories and Strategies for Change* (Cambridge, MA: MIT Press, 2004), p. 8.

20. Brophy and Wylie, adapted from "Greener Good."

21. www.Orbitz.com, pressroom.orbitz.com/ReleaseDetail.cfm?ReleaseID=244271, accessed December 19, 2007.

22. www.omsi.edu/info/pr/detail.cfm?prID=196A896D-65B3-DF53-A4DEB72 B2BD4A77A, accessed December 18, 2007.

23. www.madisonchildrensmuseum.org/about=mom/sustainability=commitment, accessed 29 April, 2008.

CASE:
Green Education in Las Vegas

In Las Vegas, promoting environmental awareness is the focus of Springs Preserve, a 180-acre attraction featuring museums, indoor and outdoor theaters, interpretive trails, xeriscape (water-wise) gardens, a children's playground, and a restaurant and shop complex that opened in June 2007. The seven new green buildings feature the largest straw-bale construction in the country (almost 42,000 square feet) and showcase evaporative cooling towers, rammed earth walls, and enough photovoltaics to power the preserve. All waste water is reclaimed on-site through bioretention ponds. Wow!

It is expected to receive LEED Platinum certification. Not surprising. What is surprising is the owner and developer of the $250 million complex: the Las Vegas Valley Water District, a public utility and non-profit agency that began providing water to the Las Vegas Valley in 1954. The district helped build the city's water delivery system and now provides water to more than 1 million people in southern Nevada.

Conceived in the late 1990s, it is seen as the right project at the right time. With Las Vegas being one of the fastest growing population centers in the country and also just about maxed out as far as water resources are concerned, educating residents about resource conservation is a no-brainer. The site was once a artesian spring that nourished "the meadows" that gave birth to Las Vegas, but the springs were all dried up by 1962. Still the site offers a beautiful landscape (listed on the National Register of Historic Places with evidence of human habitation dating back 5,000 years), and compelling history. Origen Experience is the large indoor attraction with three galleries and seventy-five exhibits with names like People of the Big Springs and Natural Mojave Gallery. There are also walking trails (including a twenty-five-acre restored cienega wetland) and the soon-to-be-completed Nevada State Museum (an independent entity sharing the campus). With programs like Rain Round-up, Water Harvesting, Clean and Green (about green cleaning products), and Introduction to Energy Conservation, the offerings revolve around helping educate the local population who are seen as the first and most important audience wave. The complex weaves together the history of the site with responsible and informed choices for today and the future. Smart synergy at work.

The Metrics

Knowing What Is Green

Science and philosophy are involved in understanding green. The science is evaluating physical impacts, devising targets, and measuring actuals. The philosophy is managing your decision making. How green do you go? Which trade-offs do you accept? Which options make the most sense?

We said it earlier, but it is worth repeating: there are degrees of green; and there are green wannabes. Learning to distinguish among them all is important. Green is today's generic term for environmentally better practice, but specifically, green refers to products and behaviors that are environmentally benign, while sustainable means practices that rely on renewable or reusable materials and processes that are green or environmentally benign. Green is akin to "do no harm"; and sustainable is comparable to "do no harm and keep the patient alive."

People and Systems Integration

Greening your institution is not just about architecture and engineering of buildings and the details of purchasing and cleaning supplies; it has to do with people. It has been said that museum professionals are among the most creative and engaged workforce, and therefore are perfectly suited to take this on. Yet green does not happen in a vacuum. Sometimes the staff get charged up about environmentalism and begin a program only to see it fizzle. Oregon Museum of Science and Industry's (OMSI) senior business analyst Damien Francaviglia leads their Sustainability Team. While he is both "overwhelmed and excited" by the task, he advises others to not bite off too much, saying, "It is better to do something and sustain it." One large science museum had to stop recycling in their food service area after realizing the time-sink in sorting plastics from paper from food. The staff time for sorting was not fully calculated and integrated into the institution's planning and budgeting. As they rethink the situation, the staff has seen puzzled guests in the food court—who are used to recycling—wondering where to put their plastics and why isn't a science museum recycling?

To be successful we need to integrate green action with the culture and systems of the museum, or we risk wasting money, time, and enthusiasm. Certainly that is no one's intended outcome. While Francaviglia and others acknowledge there is an urgency around going green, they repeat the advice to be realistic about getting things done, and find the synergies in what other people are already doing (e.g., collaborations, partnerships, and buying consortia), and engage in staff training and performance measurement and evaluation.

Winterthur Museum and Country Estate is just at the beginning of measuring where they are on environmental issues and figuring out where to go. With 1,000 acres of natural and designed landscape, over 85,000 fine and decorative art objects, and an important library collection of 60,000 volumes of rare and fine books, and over a million manuscripts and photographs as well as institutional archives and ephemera, the challenges are significant. John Castle, director of facilities services, is starting with measuring energy use on campus and polling staff about current practices. These vary by department but range from reusing scrap paper, collection housing, and retail packing materials to recycling cans, bottles, and paper, and switching over to compact fluorescent bulbs. The Conservation Department is mindful about disposing of chemical waste. The Facilities Department recovers refrigerant from old equipment, and recycles tires, oil, and batteries. An engineer by training, Castle knows the value of taking a measured approach: "We are going in small steps, to be sure we do not overreach." Still, the poll revealed many green actions already being driven by staff and a willingness to do more. As one staffer put it, "I know being green can be a pain sometimes … but I am usually happy to have a little inconvenience for a good cause. I think others would agree."

Integration is a big concept with environmental folks. In this case, integration means coordinating different systems and processes, including making adaptations, so that together they produce the most efficient, environmentally sensitive result. Understanding and promoting the integration of and synergies between systems—natural, social, and built—is the key to sustainability.

In construction and renovation, integrating building systems is key. Smart lighting systems can shut off when a room is unoccupied, or dim with available daylight to reduce energy consumption. Daylighting in turn affects heating and cooling loads and the design of your HVAC system. Water use reduction, stormwater management, and on-site wastewater management affects the designs of your parking lots and walkways, landscape, and toilet systems. None can be designed in isolation. Integrating the architectural design with the engineering design of mechanical, electrical, plumbing, and fire protection systems, for example, and civil engineering design with landscape design, is the best road to green. Make integration a key requirement in your request for qualification proposals. Select architects, engineers, and landscape designers based on the integration of their team. The traditional hegemony of the architect as artist, who expresses a building form in isolation from the engineering disciplines, is a wasteful way to design. Look for people who collaborate and innovate in an integrated fashion, a new paradigm that is transforming the architecture and engineering communities.

Many architects, engineers, and system designers innovate by studying and imitating nature's designs and processes using biomimicry, from *bios* (life) and *mimesis* (imitate). Water harvesting inspired by beetles, high-rise architecture without air conditioning inspired by the ventilation systems in termite dens, or a water- and stain-repellent textile finish that decreases the use of fluorocarbons and is based on the lotus flower are just a few examples. Important innovations grew from Leonardo da Vinci's observations of birds, and Velcro's inventor's observations of burrs on a sock. While greening museums is indeed about people, it is also about nature. Making integral connections between your departments (e.g., your facilities crew and interpretation team working together on the worm bin), and between your institution and your community (teaming up around stormwater management or energy generation or preserving open space), encourages collective and informed action.

Benchmarking and Creating a Baseline

"What gets measured gets done." We have all heard this oft-repeated phrase and there is a reason it is connected to best business practices. Evaluation and measurement are important aspects of managing change, and change is part of greening your institution. This should be welcome in the museum field's culture of evaluation and measurement: we test exhibition scripts and designs, pilot outreach programs, and evaluate the visitor experience.

Creating a baseline reflecting current practice is a good place to start. A baseline is a basic standard or level; a specific value or values that can serve as a comparison or control. By comparing and measuring their policies, practices, philosophies, and performance measures against those of high-performing organizations, museums can assess their performance and then make decisions to improve it. Stonyfield Farms, the world's leading organic yogurt maker, wants to serve as a model demonstrating that environmentally and socially responsible businesses can also be profitable. The company's approach revolves around four key principles: measure, reduce, offset, and educate. Measurement is central to goal achievement.

The International Association of Museum Facilities Administrators (IAMFA) conducts an annual benchmarking study that measures cost centers such as utilities, custodial services, grounds maintenance, security, and other issues such as the existence of a Disaster Recovery Plan.[1] Winterthur's John Castle is on the steering committee, and ninety-eight institutions from six countries participate in the study's data gathering and comparative analysis. IAMFA has formed a committee to consider ways to quantify and label museum buildings by their level of environmental sustainability. The idea for such a system grew from the European Union's Energy Performance of Buildings Directive (EPBD), legislation aimed at reducing CO_2 emissions. The directive requires all buildings occupied by a public authority or visited by large numbers of people to display an energy certificate, graded A through G relative to its energy consumption (as of this writing, the EPBD is being expanded to include all commercial buildings as well). Interestingly, the directive's preamble states that these buildings "should set an example by taking environmental and energy considerations into account."[2] Example setting is one very important step toward collective engagement and action on climate change.

To be a trusted example you need to be able to quantify your performance. There are multiple rating systems and interactive tools online and there is a growing consultancy field aimed at helping businesses and institutions audit, develop baselines, and benchmark their energy and environmental performance. You can audit just about anything: energy use, water consumption, waste and recycling, daylight levels, traffic levels, lighting use, consumption of supplies. Remember, you are measuring consumption, not costs, since costs change. Try running through a Leadership in Energy and Environmental Design for Existing Buildings (LEED-EB) checklist available at the U.S. Green Building Council (USGBC) website, or many other "how green are you" checklists, to give you your first ideas of what areas to consider. Online you will also find checklists for green restaurants and offices, even green marinas if you have water access. Use them to familiarize yourself with the categories of greening and with steps to increase your green quotient. The Resources section of the book lists some, and you may find other useful ones by searching the Web.

As you develop audit and assessment experience, branch out to the areas more specific to your institution or more advanced eco-friendliness. You may start with the low-hanging fruit of energy use reduction through energy-efficient lightbulbs, appliances, and electronics and by tightening the building envelope. Move up the ladder by getting the institution recycling, reducing paper and water consumption, and reducing chemical use, then progress to issues of sourcing products for your collections care (living and nonliving), and researching life cycle issues for all your materials.

You can use the LEED checklists as a matrix whether or not you have any interest in ever being a LEED-certified site. The checklists are not complicated, but the language may be very new to you. The value is in the concepts of systematically assessing areas of operations while acknowledging and valuing the gains from synergy. The checklists will help you sort through the building sustainability options: energy and water efficiency, site planning and use, air quality and comfort, and materials uses.

The LEED-EB reference guide is the LEED handbook for certifying existing buildings. It costs about $200 to buy from the USGBC. You can buy a similar version for new construction (LEED-NC). It explains the philosophy of, and requirements for, sustainable practices, in ways you can implement regardless of your thoughts about LEED. For example, the section on indoor chemical and pollution control explains how to reduce the need for cleaning solutions simply by increasing the size and form of walk-off mats and grates at your entrance and exit doors. The less grit and mud your staff and visitors track in, the less mopping and sweeping you have to do. That reduces the cleaning chemicals you use and the person-hours you spend. Purchasing bulk cleaning solutions and using careful mixing measurements reduces product packaging in your waste stream. This reduces waste and consumption of cleaning products, and therefore cost. Synergy.

When you create your sustainability action plan, you can assign some responsibilities to staff members and plan to contract others to outside professionals. A review by your utility provider may identify some areas where an engineer can help you make systems changes now or in the future. You can hire a LEED Accredited Professional (AP) or any other professional committed to energy efficiency and other sustainable practices to assess your facilities and help you make changes initially or on an ongoing basis. They can help with basic information—from finding out if your HVAC system is working the way it was designed to operate—to changing all your air handlers to variable frequency drives and your lights to motion-sensitive systems. Some of it you will do yourself and some will require backup. If you do hire backup, be sure that they train your staff as part of the agreement. This can reduce carrying costs of professional services but improve institutional performance and staff participation. If you do not know how to assess your heating system, your other utilities, or your waste stream, ask your contractor or service provider to help. Your utility company will do a free audit. Your waste hauler and your other sales people can give you sales records.

Careful record keeping and reporting will form the basis of your assessment. Monthly, quarterly, or annual comparisons to goals will let you know your degrees of success. Rewarding staff for performance can be as simple as a free lunch for the department with the greatest waste reduction; green hero recognition for the employee with the most innovative green solution; or free personal days for every thirty days of carpooling or using public transportation. Be creative; it is a hallmark of progress in environmental sustainability.

If you are involved in a major construction project or an assessment and upgrade of an existing building, it will be important to have an architect or engineer who is a LEED AP participating from the beginning. LEED AP is a voluntary professional certification earned by examination through USGBC. It guarantees the museum that the other consultant has passed the exam for competency in energy efficiency and sustainable building practices. This does not cover every aspect of green institutional behavior, but does address the building and site issues that are a huge part of your greening project. Whether or not you pursue LEED certification, a LEED professional will provide the expertise you need to create a green building. The USGBC website lists LEED AP professionals.

Will we have lots of LEED-certified museums? We do not know. Certification is not as important as working toward best practice. Not every building will be certified, or any other LEED level, but the process and principles can help you significantly reduce your negative impact on the environment while containing or reducing your operating costs. Remember too, as one engineer put it, "Going green is a little like living a healthy lifestyle. It's an ongoing process; not like 'going on a diet' where you lose weight and that's it. You need to continually measure and adjust or you will just revert back to old habits and gain the weight back." OMSI reviews its CO_2 emissions and solid waste on a monthly basis along with other performance metrics as part of the organization's triple bottom line assessment.

Carbon Footprint

Carbon footprint is generally understood to be "a measure of the impact human activities have on the environment in terms of the amount of greenhouse gases produced, measured in units of carbon dioxide."[3] There are calculators online to measure your institution's carbon footprint, again to serve as a benchmark against which you can go about identifying reductions in carbon emissions or mitigating them through purchasing offsets. You can measure your direct or primary footprint, which is CO_2 emissions from burning fossil fuels (energy use and transportation) and your indirect or secondary footprint, which is CO_2 emissions from the whole life cycle of products we use. So when you pursue energy efficiency and encourage carpooling, teleconferencing, and use of public transport, and source locally to cut transportation of goods, you are working toward reducing your direct carbon footprint. When you recycle and in turn use recycled content products, when you consider the environmental impact in the production of the items you use (ask the manufacturer; many have measures), you are on your way to reducing your secondary footprint.

The Trustees of Reservations (The Trustees) is the oldest regional land conservation organization in the country (figure 2.1). It owns, manages,

FIGURE 2.1. Lead by example. The Trustees of Reservations' Doyle Conservation Center is a research and training facility designed to house planning, geographical information systems, ecology, and land protection staff and to build capacity for conservation in Massachusetts. The center is also used frequently for meetings and conferences by outside groups. With LEED Gold, the center is a showcase of renewable energy and sustainable building and landscape strategies that reflect the ethics of the people who work there every day and make visible the conservation mission of the organization. Copyright © Dan Gair / Blinddogphoto.com

and interprets nearly 25,000 acres on ninety-six reservations, including four National Historic Landmarks, a National Natural Landmark, and seven properties listed with the National Register of Historic Places. The organization's strategic plan emphasizes the need to provide leadership in developing a "suite of strategies that address climate change."[4] The Trustees also understand the need for measurements. Jim Younger, director of structural resources and technology, has just issued a Request for Proposals (RFP) for an audit of the organization's carbon footprint. While they have a LEED Gold building that is a showcase of renewable energy and sustainable building and landscape strategies, the organization is also far-flung across the state of Massachusetts in 250 buildings, some of them important historic structures. They want to move toward carbon neutrality and are starting with a systematic measure of carbon footprint in building energy use, transportation (they own and operate a fleet of vehicles), and recycling across all areas.

Energy Audits

The list of online tools for measuring or predicting energy efficiency can be overwhelming. Some are for buildings in the design phase; some are for buildings in use; and some lead to different kinds of accreditation. The bottom line is that you do not have to use any, but each does have particular value. Here is a brief overview, but please reassess this information when you are ready to make a decision: the field of energy efficiency is evolving so rapidly that the programs could change dramatically by the time you use them.

For buildings in the design phase, your design team may want to use Target Finder, an Energy Star online tool for the design of projects, renovations, or new construction developed by the U.S. Environmental Protection Agency (EPA). The engineers can assess how well the building is designed to perform compared to target performance levels for similar buildings. It is a formative evaluation. Based on the report, you can adjust your systems and procedures to achieve a different result—all in the design phase, not after you have built it.[5] Caution: Target Finder does not cover all building types. It is primarily focused on major asset types—office, industrial, retail. More unique buildings such as some museums, historic sites, zoos, aquariums, and so on may not find it conducive to use Target Finder to establish an accurate baseline and target. It can certainly be useful, but it can also be misleading if not well understood.

For existing buildings, you can plug your energy and water bills into Portfolio Manager, also on the Energy Star website. Use this online tool to track and assess energy and water consumption for your entire site.

Of course there is another you should know about: ASHRAE 90.1. ASHRAE is the American Society of Heating, Refrigerating and Air-Conditioning Engineers. Their 90.1 program establishes the minimum standards for saving energy and is the basis for many state and local codes.[6] These codes are enforceable whereas LEED is not. At this writing, however, USGBC and ASHRAE are in discussions around bringing basic LEED certification in line with code standards. Energy efficiency standards are rapidly changing since we are all raising the energy savings bar for ourselves, but in the meantime, ASHRAE 90.1 is what your HVAC advisors will use as the bottom line for energy efficiency. Of course it is not quite the same as the EPA ratings, but all these programs help you design and monitor an energy efficient building.

To benchmark energy costs for your existing building, gather two years of utility bills and plug them into the Portfolio Manager online tool through the Energy Star website.[7] Once you have the data recorded and graphed, you can use it as a benchmark to make comparisons to similar physical plants and identify where you might make improvements. As you reduce your energy use, you can compare the new results to past years and demonstrate your successes. The Statement of Performance that you print out is a LEED-EB requirement.

As part of your sustainability practices, Bill Gilmore, vice president of facilities at Chesapeake Bay Maritime Museum, says make it a habit—no, a rule—that the facilities manager audit and approve all utility bills. No more just paying the bill because you have to, or letting it go right to the bookkeeper because it has to get paid. One museum found that not only was it being charged for two fixtures neither it nor the utility could locate, but that the museum was being charged taxes.

Just as you should look carefully at your utility bills and measure where you are relative to energy use, a flag should be raised if consumption spikes or if over time you see a steady increase. Just as going green is not a one-shot deal, your systems need continual evaluation and tweaking to make sure they are working. That is where commissioning comes in.

Building commissioning was originally associated with the postconstruction review of HVAC systems to ensure they were properly specified and installed. That function has been expanded to include almost any building system and today commissioning agents are being included on project teams from the first day. This benefits the entire design and construction process by ensuring that the project documentation reflects the designer's and owner's intentions; inspecting the installation of systems during construction; conducting performance tests after construction; and participating in building and operation training. Commissioning is a requirement for

LEED certification. More owners, architects, and engineers are welcoming this third party set of eyes and expertise on the project team to save money and headaches as systems become more sophisticated and automated. Commissioning a new building can cost from 30 to 90 cents per square foot; this is offset by reduced energy costs, improvements to users' comfort and productivity, and reduced "rework" costs. On average, the simple payback for building commissioning is about three to four years.[8]

Retrocommissioning (sometimes also called energy audit) can also save on aspirin as facilities managers struggle with systems that are not performing as expected. The Montclair Art Museum was concerned about its energy bills and contracted with an architect and engineer to conduct a comprehensive energy master plan. The study, which looked at systems as well as architectural issues, was funded by a $25,000 grant from the New Jersey State Council on the Arts. The process of undertaking the study was a chance for staff and board members to learn about the green museums movement and what it might mean for them to take a leadership role in their community. One recommendation was for the museum to undergo retrocommissioning of its mechanical systems to identify inefficiencies and determine where upgrades might show payback.

What about energy service companies (ESCOs)? They are in the business of auditing building or preferably whole-campus energy consumption and recommending a comprehensive suite of energy-saving measures that range from better lighting and occupancy sensors to boiler replacements and fuel switching, to negotiating energy rates with utilities. Their services are commonly used in the public sector but can be used in the private sector too. Some utilities offer this type of service as well. The physical improvements they recommend are evaluated on a life cycle cost basis and the most economical improvements that fit within the client's investment payback period are selected. The ESCO handles physical improvements and is responsible for achieving stated energy performance. They are typically paid through a guarantee of energy savings from the retrofits so the upfront cost to the client is much less than if they undertook measures themselves. ESCOs also guarantee a level of energy savings and monitor facility performance to maintain it.[9]

After the Chesapeake Bay Foundation built their Philip Merrill Center and moved in, they audited their energy use. Audits are important if the building is new or old, and you do not stop doing them just because you had the building commissioned. Nothing tells you about how you use the building better than an audit. They reviewed lighting, then heating, plug loads, and cooling. They found that daylighting was reaching further into the building than they had anticipated, making it worthwhile to place sensors on more lights than they had originally. And they were stunned at the plug load they were carrying. How many printers, CPUs, monitors, lights, electric staplers, pencil sharpeners, faxes, phones, copiers, scanners, and cell phone chargers do you have plugged into the walls of your office, your department, and your museum? One of the best, first activities of your green team may be a room-by-room audit of what you have, what you use, and what you do. Knowing what you have and what you pay for is an often-overlooked method of becoming more efficient.

Waste Stream Audits

Just like an energy audit, a waste audit is an assessment of how much waste you pay for—yes, pay for—and why. The audit helps you evaluate the costs of waste removal: your hauling and disposal fees (average costs can be $75 per ton); and labor, container, and equipment costs. Then as you manage and reduce, by either producing less or reusing materials, and by diverting unavoidable waste from the landfills through composting, recycling, or sale, you can track the savings and look for income opportunities. Since sustainability efforts always consider full-cycle costs, not one-time costs, valuing the hidden costs of labor, container, and space helps you understand the true values and costs of both the old way and the new.

The New York State Association for Reduction, Reuse and Recycling (NYS3R) website, in its business category, has a great waste audit section. The forms lead you through the math of measuring and costing your waste. That means you estimate your average weekly or monthly weights (tons) of refuse—recycled or thrown away—based on your inspection of containers and their contents. Then you calculate the costs to haul away that amount. It requires significant staff time to conduct an audit, but the results will help you truly understand the cost of throwing away anything—and it might surprise you. For example, what would it cost if there were less garbage to haul? How does a decrease in garbage and a corresponding increase in recycling affect the costs? What are the break points? Now that you have your benchmark, how much can you reduce your waste and recycling based on thoughtful practices in purchasing and production throughout the museum? By tracking your waste and your recycling after the initial audit, you can document your success.

Life Cycle Analysis: Construction and Daily Use

What does green cost? Objective studies have confirmed that energy efficient construction is not necessarily more expensive than conventional construction: "there is no significant difference in average cost for green buildings as compared to non-green buildings."[10] For capital construction there are metrics and tools to measure return on investment (ROI). When measuring capital construction costs, the balance between up-front costs, which simply measure initial price, and life cycle costs is important. You can do a life cycle cost analysis to calculate whether a specific project—renovation with systems upgrade, a major addition, or a new building—is worth the initial investment. Your integrated design team should be able to help you determine the total costs associated with a capital construction over its lifetime.[11] The analysis considers such factors as:

❖ Purchase or construction costs
❖ Fuel costs
❖ Operation, maintenance, and repair costs
❖ Replacement costs
❖ Resale or disposal costs
❖ Loan interest payments
❖ Nonmonetary benefits (productivity, health, comfort, reduced absenteeism, and well-being of occupants)

If you are not building or renovating, does life cycle analysis apply? It certainly does. You can assess the products and materials you use for the office, special events, public programs, exhibit design—everything. What is the life cycle of that boardroom chair? Where did its materials come from and how were they harvested and manufactured? How were the pieces assembled? How did the chair get to the seller and then to you? What packaging and transportation is required in all of those activities? Then how does it affect the air quality or the floor surfaces in the boardroom? When you dispose of it, how will that affect the environment?

LEED Program

The USGBC's LEED Program has become a widely accepted method for measuring environmental impact of buildings. LEED has become a nationally accepted benchmark for green building design and construction. To date there are hundreds of certified projects and the LEED brand is understood in the marketplace as an imprimatur of green value. Many colleges and universities use LEED as a standard for capital construction as do dozens of municipalities and some states. Museums with LEED certification are growing in number and many are proud to proclaim that they are the first in their category (art museum, children's museum, etc.) or in their state or city to achieve certification.

The USGBC website is a storehouse full of valuable information, Powerpoints, and downloads of publications, data, and tools. Anyone interested in learning more about sustainable building and site practices should start there. In brief, here are the program basics:

> The rating system evaluates a building and site; points are awarded in six areas.
>
> 1. sustainable site
> 2. water efficiency
> 3. energy and atmosphere
> 4. materials and resources
> 5. indoor environmental quality
> 6. innovation and design process
>
> There are four progressive levels of certification based on the number of points awarded (Certified, Silver, Gold, and Platinum).
>
> There are currently six systems, and tailored systems are being developed for building types within these categories for retail, health care, and schools: New Construction (LEED-NC), Existing Buildings (LEED-EB), Commercial Interiors (LEED-CI), Core and Shell Development (LEED-CS), Neighborhood Development (LEED-ND), and Homes (LEED-H).

As of this writing the LEED program is undergoing significant revision. Changes were expected to roll out in 2008 in which the separate rating systems above (LEED-NC, LEED-EB, etc.) would be merged into one overall LEED system with a bookshelf approach to credits, creating in essence a custom rating system for each specific building that is tied to its use and geography. For example, a credit for water conservation in New Jersey is very different from a water conservation credit in Arizona. These changes are in part a response to charges that the existing rating systems were too rigid. This change is expected to make the system more flexible and adaptable and support the USGBC's goal of 100,000 certified buildings by 2010. The expectation is this will be a boon for museums and for historic preservation, building types with specialized needs unlike buildings in other sectors.

To LEED or not to LEED? If that is a question you are considering, we suggest going back to metrics and measurements: assess the full value of the process, not just the cost. LEED is a measurable brand that is generally recognized as a rigorous measure of building performance and environmental impact. Each institution will make its decision for different reasons.

Many owners choose to use the LEED guidelines as a tool for designing buildings but elect not to go for certification (sometimes you hear the phrase "LEED Certifiable") but those in the industry are wary of greenwashing, knowing of course that having a measure is very often the best way to ensure accountability and actual monetary and environmental payback on green. As one seasoned mechanical engineer put it, "LEED holds your feet to the fire." Those who have been in the capital project trenches know that every building project, whether new construction or renovation, has budget crunches as one moves through the project phases from schematic design through construction administration. We will talk more about project budgets and scheduling in chapter 3 but the take-away message here is the value of measurement. Establishing a green goal on day one, sharing the responsibility for your green goal as well as your budget with your integrated team, and having objective measurements of both are proven methods for project success.[12]

What does LEED certification cost? That question is frequently asked of architects and project managers and the answer is, "It depends." Designing and building the project is one thing. Getting LEED certified is another and while concern has been expressed about the cost of documentation and critique of the LEED certification process as cumbersome and expensive, the fact is the costs to achieve actual certification are coming down as teams become accustomed to the requirements and as the USGBC has responded to critiques and rolled out changes to the program. Since 2006 all LEED documentation is online and it can be done in steps with a design phase submittal and a construction phase submittal. Prior to streamlined documentation, project teams had to submit binders with reams of paper at the conclusion of the project, and a 2002 study indicated that the LEED certification process cost anywhere from $10,000 to $60,000.[13] This was enough to turn some people off and led to rumblings about the value of LEED certification. Today, as the entire green design and construction industry has moved forward at a dazzlingly rapid pace, those costs have gone down.[14]

Another word about costs. We have already cited the seminal study reporting that new green buildings are on average not more expensive than new traditional buildings. There will be green components and practices of new and existing buildings that cost more or less than business as usual. It may be tempting to highlight costs of new technology as unnecessary add-ons, but if the planning process is integrated, no single cost is responsible for cost overruns or savings. Any cost can be attributed to a decision. Budget crunches happen for all sorts of reasons: since the budget is connected to the schedule, delayed decision making by the owner, late orders by the contractor, and supply delays can add costs. Economic conditions and trade policies can affect prices.

Value engineering is the place where projects can lose green value. Since green design is all about integration, cutting one item to save money very often will compromise another item, thereby costing you either reductions in energy savings or in postoccupancy fixes later on. Again, measurements and evaluation are key. Value engineering sometimes is necessary but the ideal is to preplan and work together as an integrated team to continually align green goals with project budget, schedule, and quality (smart teams now include a construction manager to advise early on constructability and scheduling issues). The ideal is to design to a budget all along and to eliminate value engineering, where very often all the best design elements are cut, and replaced in a hurry with subpar substitutes, and where quality and green results are compromised—surely not your desired outcome.

Other Metrics, Tools, and Systems

The U.S. Department of Energy's (DOE) website and its High Performance Buildings Database are excellent resources for learning more about best practices.[15] We have already mentioned the Energy Star site (a joint program of the DOE and the EPA) with software tools and analysis programs. The High Performance Buildings Database is a wonderful resource for learning about built projects. Currently ninety-six projects worldwide are included in the searchable database (you can search by project name, owner, location, building type, and size). The information on each project is comprehensive and offers a valuable opportunity to learn from built work. Each case study includes details, data, and stories in the following areas:

✤ Process
✤ Finance
✤ Land use
✤ Site and water
✤ Energy
✤ Materials
✤ Indoor environment
✤ Rating and awards
✤ Images
✤ Lessons

Green Globes (GG) is an environmental assessment and rating system that was developed by the Green Building Initiative (GBI) and grew out of the UK's Building Research Establishment's Environmental Assessment Method (BREEAM). Green Globes for new construction was adapted from a system that is widely used in Canada, where it is one of only two green building rating systems recognized by the Canadian federal government. Under the trade name Go Green Comprehensive, it is also the basis of the Building Owners and Managers Association of Canada's national energy and environmental program for existing buildings.[16] The system entered the United States in 2004. It operates on a percentage ranking system, awarding one to four globes. Assessments cover the following areas:

- ❖ Management
- ❖ Site
- ❖ Energy
- ❖ Water
- ❖ Resources
- ❖ Emissions
- ❖ Indoor environment

The William J. Clinton Presidential Center is a 150,000-square-foot building located in Little Rock, Arkansas. The building achieved two Green Globes for its use of environmentally sensitive systems and low-impact materials as well as the reuse of a previously underutilized industrial area. The Clinton Library has also achieved LEED-EB. There has been critique of Green Globes around its financial sponsorship from industry groups (a potential conflict of interest), lack of transparency in decision making, and flaws in its online tools.[17] Like LEED, Green Globes has been responding to feedback. It is diversifying its funding base and has made improvements to its online tools. The perceived competition between the LEED system and Green Globes is in many ways a red herring. When asked about what seems to be acrimony between adherents of one system or another, one green engineer waved it off by saying, "People should use what they are comfortable with; some rating system is better than no rating system."

In 2006 the Living Building Challenge was launched by the Cascadia Region Green Building Council, the Pacific Northwest Chapter of the USGBC that encompasses Oregon, Washington, and British Columbia. With the tag line, "Imagine buildings that are built to operate as elegantly and efficiently as a flower," the system is based on a series of prerequisites, each of which must be met to comply. The sixteen prerequisites are clustered in six categories:

- ✤ Site design
- ✤ Energy
- ✤ Materials
- ✤ Water
- ✤ Indoor environmental quality
- ✤ Beauty and inspiration

Ratings are conferred after a project has been operating for a year and are based on what a building has done rather than what it is projected to do. The project founders felt compelled to release the challenge "to provide a signal to the green building industry where it needs to head in the next few years if we are to address the daunting challenges ahead."[18] They also stress that the system is not meant to compete with LEED; rather, they see it as supporting LEED goals by raising the bar to encourage owners and design teams to vision to "think beyond Platinum." Further, the founders point out,

Several things have transpired in the short time since LEED 1.0 emerged that put the Living Building Standard in context:

- ✤ LEED has been adopted at a far greater rate than anyone's expectations and has begun to transform the whole building industry. LEED has continued to evolve and improve and many municipalities have adopted LEED Silver as a baseline standard.
- ✤ Multiple Platinum buildings have emerged around the country and some with zero or small first-cost premiums, signaling that the market is ready to move beyond Platinum in the near future.
- ✤ The USGBC has begun to explore the idea of LEED V3.0 as a major restructuring of how its system works. The specifics have not yet been determined and the implementation timeline is likely another one to two years.
- ✤ Zero energy and zero waste water buildings are beginning to emerge around the country and the cost of wind, solar, and

> other sustainable technologies continues to drop just as it is becoming clear that we are past the point of peak oil and cheap energy. Carbon neutral construction of buildings will no doubt follow.
>
> ✤ Most significantly, it is clear that major environmental trends such as climate change are directly linked to human resource use and from the building industry itself. The rate of change and potential disastrous scenarios for our communities and quality of life are increasing. It is also clear that public opinion is finally awakening to that reality as evidenced by the shift in mass media attention of the issue, the Clinton Climate Initiative, the Mayor's Climate Initiative, the 2030 challenge, and governmental efforts led by the State of California.[19]

As of this writing, a draft "Living Site and Infrastructure Challenge" has been issued with the charge that "not only do our buildings need to be 'living,' so too must the spaces between. What would it mean to design a living roadway? A living park or pier? A living plaza or playground?"[20] The Living Building and Site Challenges are very exciting developments underscoring the urgency around collective and concerted action on addressing climate change issues. Stay tuned as built work emerges using this system and consider reaching high as you approach any new building developments.

Accreditation

Aside from enforceable codes for energy efficiency, air quality, and water use, green building practices are primarily a voluntary pursuit. Yet, for reasons we have already outlined, museums would do well to heed the green call. Indeed, recently revised accreditation standards for zoos and aquariums state, "Interpretive programs and publications should include information on the conservation of wildlife and their habitats to foster concern for disappearing biodiversity and to elevate the environmental knowledge of individuals in the field, in the zoo, and the visiting public. … The institution should demonstrate responsible energy and natural resource conservation through such activities as recycling, water conservation initiatives … and use of solar energy."[21] American Association of Museums (AAM) accreditation may well follow suit. Carol Enseki, president of the Brooklyn Children's Museum, member of the AAM board, and also on the Accreditation Visiting Committee, says, "I can see future AAM accreditation criteria dealing with sustainability. A good aspect of planning is how to improve energy efficiency, which of course frees dollars to go towards programs and services."[22]

Freeing dollars for programs and services? That sounds a lot like the kind of sustainability that funders refer to when assessing an organization's capacity and ability to continue to pursue its mission for the long term. Environmental sustainability and fiscal sustainability are very much linked and are meaningful, when measured, to those from whom you seek support. We will cover money issues later but suffice to say metrics—that is measurement and evaluation—are key to achieving green and to demonstrating its value to the long-term health of the organization, its staff, and its collections, as well as its benefit to the community.

Notes

1. For information about the museum benchmarking survey, visit www.iamfa .org.

2. Andrew Warren, "The Energy Performance of Buildings Directive—A Summary of Its Objectives and Contents," Chartered Institute of Building Service Engineers briefing note, www.euroace.org/reports/CIBSE_EUBD.pdf, accessed December 15, 2007.

3. www.carbonfootprint.com/carbonfootprint.html, accessed December 14, 2007.

4. www.thetrustees.org/index.cfm, accessed December 15, 2007.

5. www.energystar.gov/index.cfm?c=evaluate_performance.bus_portfoliomanager#tools, accessed December 10, 2007.

6. www.ashrae.org, accessed December 10, 2007.

7. Energy Star is a joint program of the U.S. Environmental Protection Agency and the U.S. Department of Energy geared toward saving money and protecting the environment through energy efficient products and practices. The program's website is a bountiful resource for data and energy saving strategies and resources for institutions and businesses as well as homeowners. www.energystar.gov.

8. www.energydesignresources.com/resource/17/, accessed December 15, 2007.

9. Many thanks to Aaron Binkley, AIA LEED AP, for this text on ESCOs.

10. Davis Langdon, "Cost of Green Revisited: Reexaming the Feasibility and Cost Impact of Sustainable Design in the Light of Increased Market Adoption," July 2007, www.davislangdon.com/upload/images/publications/USA/The%20Cost%20of%20 Green%20. Revisited .pdf, accessed 29 April, 2008.

11. The Building Life-Cycle Cost Program (BLCC 5.3-07) is a program developed by the National Institute of Standards and Technology (NIST) to provide computational support for the analysis of capital investments in buildings. www1.eere .energy.gov/femp/information/download_blcc.html.

12. Geof Syphers, Arnold M. Sowell Jr., Ann Ludwig, and Amanda Eichel, "Managing the Cost of Green Buildings," August 2003.

13. N. Howard and R. Watson, "Special LEED Section: An Update on LEED 2.1," *Environmental Design and Construction*, July 12, 2002.

14. Langdon, "Cost of Green Revisited."

15. www.eere.energy.gov/buildings/highperformance/.

16. www.thegbi.org/home.asp.

17. Gail Brager and Corinne Benedek, "Examining Rating Systems: A Look at Green Globes,"University of California–Berkeley, www.aia.org/nwsltr_cote.cfm?page-name=cote_a_0703_GG, accessed December 16, 2007.

18. www.cascadiagbc.org/lbc/Lb-challenge-v1-2, accessed December 16, 2007.

19. www.cascadiagbc.org/lbc/Lb-challenge-v1-2, accessed December 16, 2007.

20. www.cascadiagbc.org/lbc/living-site-1.0.pdf, accessed December 16, 2007.

21. Association of Zoos and Aquariums, *Accreditation Standards and Related Policies*, 2007.

22. Adapted from Sarah Brophy and Elizabeth Wylie, "Being Green: Museums in the Green Movement," *Museum News*, September–October 2006.

CASE:
The Getty Center and LEED-EB

When we all experienced an endowment reality check during the stock market decline in the early 2000s, any museum with significant stock holdings felt a pinch on resources. At the Getty Center, the reduction in portfolio value triggered budget reductions (figure 2.2). Energy bills, again being any institution's second largest cost (behind payroll), were a prime target. Addressing those costs set the scene for welcoming and pursuing LEED-EB certification.

We Can Do That!

When James L. Bullock, director of facilities at The Getty Center, attended the 2004 annual conference of APPA, formerly the Association of Physical Plant Administrators, now Leadership in Educational Facilities, he sat in on a session on LEED-EB. As he listened he kept thinking "we do that" and "we can do that." He contacted the presenter and invited her for a visit and discussion with senior staff to gauge whether or not The Getty Center had the chance to become certified without any major renovations. They agreed that it could, based on existing conditions, but with some modifications and some serious efforts to document processes and building performance. They agreed to apply for certification in time for an upcoming International Facility Manager Association (IFMA) Best Practices Forum being held at The Getty Center. They had six weeks to get the paperwork done—that meant a near-heroic effort.

Like others who have done this, Joseph May, manager of maintenance, planning, and support at The Getty Center, describes the process as a journey. There is a learning curve, small or huge depending upon your background. It is an institution-wide process involving leadership, facilities managers, custodial management, program and exhibits staff, and grounds management. It extends to your relationship with city services, utilities, vendors, suppliers, and visitors. For example, The Getty Center recycles 47 percent of its waste, which earns it an extra credit in the LEED process, but the effort requires full staff education and participation. "It really is an all-hands deal," May says.

The Getty Center was able to complete certification with little extra cost, because the thoughtful work had been done during design

FIGURE 2.2. Green roofs and chaparral. That is not what leaps to mind when you think of The Getty Center. They were, however, part of the mix of sustainable practices enabling the center to complete certification with little extra cost. Thoughtful work during design and construction, and careful record keeping on energy and water usage, cleaning procedures and chemical usage, and waste management since opening, dramatically shortened the pathway to their LEED goal. Photo by John Paul Stephens © 2000 J. Paul Getty Trust

and construction, and in such a phenomenally short time, because of that thoughtful work all along: record keeping on energy and water usage, cleaning procedures, chemical usage, and waste management. They had already reduced irrigation on the hillside, begun changing out incandescent lightbulbs for compact fluorescents, and had existing energy efficiency measures such as carbon monoxide monitors in the parking garage for on-demand ventilation only instead of twenty-four-hour ventilation. Still, making changes and documenting them took up to 3,000 staff hours, with twenty-five staff involved to some degree. May was the "gatekeeper" for the LEED-EB process and The Getty Center used a LEED AP consultant to help. Having one involved in the certification process earns you one credit, and none of the staff were LEED APs. The added advantage was the consultant's role as the museum's advocate with USGBC.

What Do They Do?

The Getty Center is very conscious of energy efficiency, waste management, and site management, and they embrace alternative methods. They have reduced total energy consumption by 10 percent and electricity use by 15 percent. For example, a system in the information technology training room has automatic turnoffs so the instructor can shut down all computers in one action. Originally the building management system would turn on all the computers at 8 a.m and turn them off at 5 p.m. Now the instructor can turn them on just in time before classes. Achieving energy efficiency is everyone's responsibility, so giving staff responsibility and control was as important as monitoring real-time use and making adaptations to fit real work needs.

The Getty Research Institute at The Getty Center has a large library, as you can imagine. In the original construction the lights in the stacks had sensors so that as someone entered an aisle, that light would come on. The sensors were too sensitive and merely walking down the main aisle would trigger the lights in the side aisles. They took out the sensors and turned the system back to always on, but May is committed to resolving the problem and is currently testing a new sensor and fine tuning it to see if it addresses the need.

Creative Solutions to Unusual Circumstances

Even though The Getty Center is a campus of several buildings on a mountaintop, according to Los Angeles standards it is a high-rise, which meant they had to include a helicopter pad for medical emergencies. The helipad has a turf surface, and numerous rooftops are green, including the roof over the main underground parking structure, which includes a sculpture garden and water feature.

The surrounding terrain is a mountaintop with limited flat land available to work with, so parking had to go underground. So much went underground that they earned an extra credit for innovation. Ninety-nine percent may be a new record in museum underground parking. Open parking creates a heat island that disturbs microclimates. Putting the seven-level visitor parking structure underground—topped with a sculpture garden with grass, natural plantings, and decomposed granite—reduces the heat island effect.

Then there is the weather. The Santa Ana winds come from the east, off the desert, in both winter and summer. They are always very dry, and either very cold or very warm. A sophisticated computerized building management system controls zone boxes in the HVAC system, channeling warm air or cool air as needed. The air handlers monitor relative humidity of the return air and trigger an injection of steam from the boilers into the airflow. This means that The Getty Center's collections are always assured of optimum conditions even when the weather is demanding.

Recertification

The Getty Center recently submitted documents for recertification at the LEED Silver level. The center has a custodial contractor willing to switch to all Green Seal cleaners, and to implement appropriate practices that will also add LEED credits. May and his staff made time to document daylight and views that they did not during initial certification: the process requires measuring window space at every workstation. And since the ten-year-old carpeting is beginning to need replacement, it will be totally green carpet this time, which helps earn more points for a higher LEED certification level.

Why are they so committed to this? Originally they wanted acknowledgment that thoughtful decisions all these years meant they had built a LEED-quality building before LEED was a criterion. For recertification they still want to demonstrate, as Bullock says, "that we aren't just up here on the hill consuming resources." The effort has had the complete support of the board of trustees, the president, the visitors, and the neighbors. It demonstrates that The Getty Center is being a good neighbor, has long been one, and is willing to put in the effort to raise the bar for itself. With the recent certification renewal, the goal was Silver. Eventually, they will go for Gold.

CASE:
Greening Mass Audubon

On fragile Cape Cod, the Massachusetts Audubon Society (founded in 1896 to stop the slaughter of birds for use on women's fashions and today the largest conservation organization in New England with 100,000 members and stewardship for 33,000 acres) has developed a green building at its Wellfleet Bay Wildlife Sanctuary. The Esther Underwood Johnson Nature Center houses interpretive programs and exhibits, classes, a day camp, and connections to walking trails. Its photovoltaic arrays produce 21 kilowatts of energy, estimated to be 30 percent of peak demand for the buildings. Natural ventilation strategies are so effective that visitors sometimes mistakenly think the building is air-conditioned and question why a conservation group would use energy in such an extravagant way. The new gift shop is a smaller space than the former, yet the retail sales have increased—it is attributed to increased daylighting. Bob Prescott, the sanctuary's director, says that they are still teaching themselves how to teach about their green building. He feels strongly, however, about the building's potential to help sanctuary staff spread the green word: "We have a tremendous opportunity to influence people who come from all over and see this building." Meanwhile, Prescott's blog on the sanctuary's website is an ongoing source of information, engaging staff and visitors in the evolution of the green building and sharing information about sustainable practices. At this writing, the project team has submitted documentation and the building is awaiting its LEED rating, which is hoped to be Platinum.

Mass Audubon's road to green at the Wellfleet sanctuary is marked by greening efforts dating back to the 1980s when the organization already had a well-developed energy policy as well as conservation and education initiatives, and Cape Cod was covered with low-tech windmills supported by tax credits. According to Prescott, who has been with the organization twenty-five years, the New Alchemy Institute (NAI) was very influential to Mass Audubon. NAI was founded on Cape Cod in 1969 by John Todd, Nancy Jack Todd, and William McLarney. Called New Alchemists, a group of scientists and thinkers (John Todd worked at Woods Hole Oceanographic Institute) gathered on a twelve-acre former farm in Falmouth. From 1971 to 1991 they focused on green innovation in agriculture, aquaculture, and bioshelters. Todd and his colleagues devised the Living Machine, a self-contained water treatment system using ecological engineering. It does this by using diverse communities of bacteria and other microorganisms, algae, plants, trees, snails, fish, and other living creatures. NAI was a real influence locally. The innovative thinking of the group and its successor, Ocean Arks, as well as John Todd's writing and teaching, has continued to influence many others, including colleges, conservation groups, and museums. NAI's 1970s message is eerily prescient of our current situation.

> Among our major tasks is the creation of ecologically-derived human support systems—renewable energy, agriculture, aquaculture, housing and landscapes. The strategies we research emphasize a minimal reliance on fossil fuels and operate on a scale accessible to individuals, families and small groups. The urgency of our efforts is based on our belief that the industrial societies which now dominate the world are in the process of destroying it.[1]

Mass Audubon's conservation mission includes habitat conservation and one of their strategic plan goals is to reduce the ecological impact of climate change by serving as a model for energy efficiency and sustainable design. The organization has six green facilities using a range of strategies from photovoltaic arrays and passive ventilation to high-performance envelopes and rainwater collection systems. Their Saltonstall Nature Center at the Broadmoor Wildlife Sanctuary in Natick received an energy innovation award in 1985 from the U.S. Department of Energy. Distinct differences exist between that early example and the most recent Wellfleet facility: architecture and engineering teams are more savvy and the sheer availability (and affordability) of technologies and materials is promising.

Today, Mass Audubon's Green Team is focused on initiatives at their twenty staffed sites statewide:

- ⚜ Energy and water conservation
- ⚜ 1,700 compact fluorescent bulbs distributed to field sites
- ⚜ 84 refrigerators and freezers manufactured before 1985 replaced with new Energy Star models
- ⚜ 80 computer monitors replaced with energy efficient flat screens
- ⚜ 13 sites received energy audits focusing on insulation, air sealing, and lighting fixtures

- ✤ Green power purchasing: In 2006, 31 percent of the organization's total electricity consumption was from green power purchased through green power products offered by local utilities.
- ✤ Renewable energy generation: solar and wind
- ✤ Photovoltaic installations at nine sanctuaries, funded by Massachusetts Technology Collaborative (MTC), and Mass Audubon's operating budget and capital fund-raising.
- ✤ A grant from MTC has funded a study to determine the feasibility of adding a wind turbine at the Wellfleet Bay facility.

When asked what comes next, Stu Weinreb, director of capital assets and planning at Mass Audubon, says, "We are instituting green cleaning products and want to continue with energy use reduction by conservation and taking care of 'phantom loads.'" The team has also identified transportation—reducing fleet vehicle gasoline consumption—as the next frontier.

Note

1. *Bulletin of the New Alchemists*, Fall 1970, www.vsb.cape.com/~nature/ greencenter/, accessed December 18, 2007. John Todd is recognized as an innovator in ecological design, especially for his signature ecological waste treatment systems. The Todds currently live in Burlington, Vermont, and their website and blog are wonderful resources. www.oceanarks.org.

The Options

Where Does It Start?

Now you know the "why" of green, and you know where to start; but how do you start? Sometimes staff instigates green; sometimes the board does. It can be one person on a recycling mission, or a team charged with finding ways to reduce waste, save energy, and change behaviors. Maybe a manager or board member says, "We have to find a way to reduce these energy bills!" However it starts, there are two terms you will hear repeatedly from those who have gone green: *journey* and *champion*. Going green is a journey, not a destination; and you need a green champion to lead the charge. Anyone can be the champion; feel free to step up. This chapter is all about what museums are already doing; how they are integrating greening activities and finding synergies with mission, brand, finances, physical plant and site, and their policies and planning.

The sheer scale of many green museum projects may lead you to believe that more of the "big guys" have gone green than have the "little guys," but that is a matter of visibility. Sheila Sheridan, fellow and past board member of the International Facilities Management Association, points out that larger museums have a larger proportion of board members from industrial or business backgrounds where green is already considered a corporate responsibility. A larger museum may have critical mass in green leadership where a smaller institution may only have one board voice, or none, with green experience. A larger museum may have facilities maintenance staff with experience in energy efficiency or the responsibility to pursue it. Often the political environment in the state or city has set the scene for the largest museums to take leadership positions in sustainability. In Pittsburgh, the Children's Museum and the Senator John Heinz History Center are just two of the many green corporate and nonprofit institutions encouraged financially and philosophically by the Heinz Endowment. In California and Vermont, like Chicago, Portland, and Pittsburgh, the public simply expects green in buildings and operations and increasingly there are state and municipal codes that require energy and water efficiency. But it is not just big museums. The Havre De Grace Maritime Museum in Maryland is putting on a green roof; the UC Davis Design Museum has a staff of five yet it is a leader in sustainable exhibits; the Provincetown Art Association Museum's renovation and addition is residential-sized and green. Small is often greener.

With the many exciting new green museums or green additions, it is easy to think you have to build a new building to be green. Not true. Actually, not building is even greener since it conserves the embodied energy in your existing building (the energy expended to produce, transport, and use the construction materials). You avoid the waste generated by demolishing the old and constructing the new. Greening your existing building, whether it is historic or four years old, is an environmentally sustainable practice, and absolutely appropriate.

Creating a Green Team

Going green is contagious. Someone catches the bug and with a little encouragement green practices and policies begin replicating themselves. It usually starts small; someone suggests the office begin recycling paper or cardboard, and frequently mirrors what staff practice in their home.

The most effective method of pursuing sustainability in an existing building or organization is through the formation of a green team. A successful green team involves a variety of staff and board members to work, learn, and engage the rest of the institution. Considering participation in decision making and planning improves commitment, a sensible starting point begins with identifying team members' experience and interests, and then moves on to a general survey of staff and volunteers.

Green has been incorporated into all aspects of the Shedd Aquarium in Chicago since they started office recycling in 1992. Michelle Jost, conservation program manager at Shedd, began with a green team in 1996, developed a paid position in charge of green in 2004, and then was asked to lead a citywide greening initiative in 2007. Shedd's greening effort has been successfully internalized in the strategic plan and across all operations. How have they done it? Jost credits "staff initiative and engagement" for their success. The original goal, when they presented the green team idea to the executive management team, was to begin a conversation on the role of green at the aquarium. Within a month of the meeting, five vice presidents formed a new Green Steering Committee and green became a core objective for Shedd. This high level of support laid the foundation for their far-reaching and successful changes.

Green teams often begin by pursuing low-hanging fruit, such as implementing a more rigorous recycling program, and move to more complex projects—locating a local source for specific program supplies or café food. Bonnie Paganis, general manager in food services at Shedd, was composting waste by transporting it home each day. When she reached critical mass, she expanded to a green bin on-site. In the first five years of composting, Shedd diverted 75.6 tons of landfill-destined garbage (figure 3.1). While the green team is charged with looking at the practices of the organization, it often comes back to the actions of each individual.

Sustaining the work of a green team is essential to its effectiveness. Green team leadership needs to change over time as new challenges are presented. Julie Silverman, Director of New at ECHO Lake Aquarium and Science Center at the Leahy Center for Lake Champlain in Burlington, Vermont, found she needed to renew their green daily practice. In 2003 the new building and institution reopened; four years later as the building had matured, there was new staff, and there have been changes in building use and programs. The green team needed renewal. Silverman, original green champion for in-house operations, wanted to participate but felt the leadership and energy should come from others this time in order to be more of an institutional project than a personal mission. The ECHO Green Lantern Team—a rich and inspiring reference to comic heroes—was born. The new seven-member team represents all departments and strata and includes a volunteer—an excellent way to encourage communication with volunteers, elicit outside perspective, and perhaps find a bit more available time for the effort.

The ECHO team renewal began with an informal, grassroots group, and started with what people were already passionate about and already practicing: recycling paper, cardboard, glass, cans, and plastic. Surprisingly, the stepped-up recycling program did not work very well. Too many staff members were not separating recyclable materials in the bins. The team researched the problem and discovered everyone recycled at home using curbside pickup, which accepted mixed recyclables in one bin (mixed stream); but the science center's commercial pickup required separating materials (single stream). The team set about addressing the problem by asking the staff what would make recycling easier. The result? A commitment to create better signs and provide training—yes, training. Recycling is a habit and a learned behavior; doing it correctly and responsibly often requires training.

Sustainability is integrated into every aspect of Shedd Aquarium's operations. A conservation ethic permeates our culture, energizes our staff and volunteers, inspires our guests and colleagues, and is based on a vision for a global environment in which ecosystems are healthy, understood and valued.

Providing sustainable dining options to our 2 million guests poses daily challenges, which have inspired flexibility, innovation and many creative solutions.

Your organization can become more sustainable too! You may choose to replicate our best practices or you may create new and different ways of increasing sustainability. A key ingredient is a commitment to routinely assessing the overall impact of your decisions and making choices that support a healthy bottomline for your business and the environment.

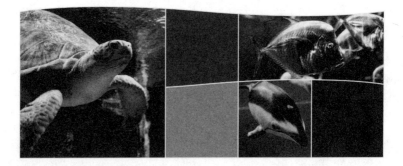

FIGURE 3.1. Education matters. Recycling is simple on the surface, but complex in practice. Good information, education, and encouragement are critical to making a recycling system work. Shedd Aquarium's staff have been asked so often for advice on how they developed their successful programs that they have created a how-to and why-to for all of us. Courtesy of Bonnie Paganis

SHEDD AQUARIUM
Sustainability Practices
Dining Options

SHEDD'S APPROACH TO WASTE MANAGEMENT:
(Reduce, Reuse, Recycle and Compost)

WHY WE REDUCE AND REUSE:

We consider a product's impact to the environment before purchasing—from dinnerware and glassware to straws and napkins. The energy and materials used and where the product or its parts will end up after use are factors that help us determine if a product is right for us. Often the more sustainable option is also the most cost effective. Savings can be achieved by budgeting upfront. Many reusable products are less expensive than disposables when the costs are factored over time.

HOW WE REDUCE AND REUSE:

- Plates & flatware in Bubblenet (Cafeteria)
- Plates, glasses, cups and flatware in Soundings (Restaurant) and catering
- Refillable salt & pepper shakers
- Bulk condiment dispensers
- Linen tablecloths and napkins in Soundings (Restaurant)

WHY WE RECYCLE:

Having a comprehensive recycling and composting program helps limit the amount of material that is destined for landfills. We are able to lessen our waste and often save money. Recycling prevents useful material from being wasted and reduces consumption of raw materials and energy.

WHAT WE RECYCLE:

- Aluminum cans
- Glass bottles
- Plastic bottles
- Used paper
- Cardboard
- Paper
- Fryer oil
- Pickle buckets
- Wine corks

WHAT WE COMPOST:

- Produce scraps
- Bread scraps
- Some napkins
- Biodegradable food containers
- Coffee grounds

FIGURE 3.1. Continued

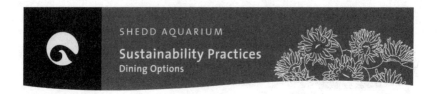

SHEDD AQUARIUM
Sustainability Practices
Dining Options

GREEN PURCHASING:

• Environmentally-friendly cleaning products

• Biodegradable straws

• Post consumer products (unbleached paper napkins
and hand towels, coffee cups and sleeves, copy paper)

• Shade grown organic coffee

• Local buying when possible

• Organic items on menu

• Soy products, including soy crayons

• Compostable containers for "grab & go" Kiosk (non-petroleum based)

• Compostable disposable service ware (plates, bowls cups and flatware)

• Energy Star Equipment

OTHER PROGRAMS:

• Staff education and awareness is part of new hire training for all
foodservice staff and annual sustainability training

• Right Bite Sustainable Seafood awareness—serving and promoting
eco-friendly seafood

• Green coffee service—washable dishes and silverware, organic shade-grown
fair-trade coffee, water and juice in pitchers, sugar bowls, cream in pitchers

• Replacing disposables with compostable products

• Staff beverage program—free refills offered when using a refillable mug
for coffee or fountain soda

• Staff meal program in reusable containers with a frequent user incentive
for returning the container

• Reusable glasses, mugs, plates and flatware for staff to borrow for use
during work hours

FIGURE 3.1. Continued

The ECHO Team have now gone beyond recycling, expanding to all sorts of operations issues. They are slowly phasing out old computer monitors for more energy efficient flat screens. The old ones get recycled, the new ones use less energy, and staff members have more room on their desks for work and trays to hold used paper that can be reloaded into a dedicated printer for in-house printing. The team is researching staple-less staples and refillable pens and has selected Green Seal products for cleaning. Someone has taken on a composting evaluation project. Once they refine the staff and volunteer process and understand the costs and benefits, they can explore scaling up the process to involve visitors in composting food products on-site. They have removed some of the lights from the vending machines to reduce electricity consumption, and a baseline electricity audit on certain equipment in the café and volunteer lounge has uncovered other ways to safely cut energy use associated with food storage and preparation. They are researching more locally produced and healthier food options, too. As they work with the utilities, the solid waste service, and the natural gas provider, they are learning what they can do to improve site sustainability; then they share it with their audience. They pass on what they learn by including an ECHO Green Lantern Tip of the Month, Green Buzz, in the science center's public electronic newsletter. They have also helped the marketing department move to using eco-ink and recycled postconsumer paper for most of their materials.

Implementation

The New England Science Center Collaborative was an early proponent of the green team concept for science centers and aquariums. Mary Lou Krambeer, former coordinator of the collaborative, sees the idea as appropriate to every kind of museum. When asked what makes a good green team, Krambeer said green team leaders have consistently identified common themes and important components:

❖ Naming a green champion as a leader and a motivator
❖ Integrating green responsibilities with existing job responsibilities (and included in annual performance reviews)
❖ Participation from all levels: staff, board, and volunteers to guarantee an integrated sustainability program
❖ Communicating green principles and actions throughout the institution and into the audience
❖ Recognizing that being green is a journey

The *green champion* is the point person responsible for advancing, monitoring, and advocating for green. This position is important enough that The Kresge Foundation requires designation of a green champion on any funding applications for support of projects with green components.

Integration with job responsibilities creates accountability. The employee is accountable to the team and supervisor for green performance, and the team and supervisor are accountable for support and encouragement of the employee's green pursuits. Integration means that fulfilling duties related to green is part of a job description, part of regular duties and responsibilities, and part of evaluation.

Participation at all levels—staff, board, and volunteers. A range of team members guarantees a variety of ideas and implementation methods, access to more collaborators and resources, a mixture of authority and opportunity for implementation, and a variety of skills and perspectives that create a functioning process. (Imagine implementing recycling goals without letting the maintenance staff in on the process or expectations.)

Broad participation on the green team solves a big part of the *communication* challenge. The rest is sharing it with non-team members. Communicating with the frontline staff and with managers, with stakeholders and the skeptics, is not just about public relations; it is basic training. Until sustainable practices are internalized by everyone, you will need to continually communicate the importance of recycling, turning off computers and lights, commuting or biking to work, conserving paper, thinking about chemicals, and so on.

The *journey* aspect comes from continual assessment. Every time we try something new we have to stop to assess the decision's environmental impact. That is time consuming and requires some expertise. That is why you focus the efforts in a green team. The team can continually assess the environmental impact of all museum actions and then make a decision to continue those actions as is or improve them.

Ask those on the green museum front how to implement a green team and they will say:[1]

- ✤ Assess current conditions then set achievement goals
- ✤ Create and implement a plan of action
- ✤ Take time to train staff and vendors
- ✤ Share your discoveries with the public
- ✤ Assess your performance and set new goals
- ✤ Recognize and reward efforts and success

Integrated Waste Management

Since so many green teams begin with recycling, we will start with waste management. Waste management means garbage, recycling, and composting, but it starts with reducing what comes into your institution and how much waste you produce. You can reduce your recycling and garbage amounts by reusing materials, selecting items that come with less packaging (more items in one box, bulk and concentrated materials), and by choosing to provide or use less. Have you noticed that more e-mails today say, "Please consider your environmental responsibility before printing this e-mail"? That is what it says at the bottom of e-mails from AAM. You will start to notice the tagline on others' messages from now on. The idea is to encourage e-mail readers to think twice before printing e-mails or their attachments. That simple tagline is a first step in managing the waste stream. Think about the environment when you go about your daily museum operations and ask questions about different practices. Can we reduce our paper consumption by changing margins on the letterhead or by managing more records and information electronically? Can we cut down on paper recycling by removing the museum from mailing lists? Can we cut down on packaging materials in the gift shop? Can we just stop buying Styrofoam?

There are two great tools to help you manage your waste stream: the mantra "reduce, reuse, recycle" and waste audits; both fit under the heading of integrated waste management. Museum staff are familiar with integrated pest management, and green builders thrive on integrated design. This follows the same concept: consider multiple techniques and tools to manage and reduce your waste. At the Oregon Museum of Science and Industry (OMSI) and museums across the country, the waste audit began with dumpster diving. The vendor's hauling records for the unsorted garbage provided the initial benchmark. The dumpster diving demonstrated that food waste and rainfall contributed significant volume and weight. Covering the dumpsters reduced weight quickly and easily. Starting worm bins for recycling food waste produced compost instead of waste and therefore reduced garbage weight and resulting hauling costs. Recycling was harder, but we will get to that later.

Waste Load Reduction

The think-before-you-print e-mail message is an example of reducing. Reduce is the first word in the mantra because reducing what you use is the most dramatic way to help the environment. You use the least energy and the fewest resources of the three Rs. If you do not produce the object or the waste, you are doing the environment a favor; but when you do use materials, the first goal is reducing what you use. You can reduce what you use, reuse and recycle what you use, compost materials, sell it, and give it away. Reduce your paper consumption with double-sided printing. It results in huge savings in paper costs and sends a message about using resources wisely. Have you ever received a direct mail from a museum, say a letter informing you of a new program, that is two single-sided pages with very few lines on the second page? The program message is potentially overshadowed by the message of waste: waste of paper (couldn't they tweak the format to fit the letter on one side or print two sided?) and waste of time (who collated those two pages, folded, and stuffed those envelopes?). Electronic communications with willing members of your audience can reduce paper use and mailing costs. Try saving and reusing single-sided printouts for drafts or in-house materials. You are reusing it, and then, of course, you can recycle it. Those are two of the easiest examples of a waste stream reduction process from your own desk, and together they are the simplest form of integrated waste management.

ECHO's Green Lantern Team is tackling paper reduction. The benchmark is the office supplier's records for museum purchases for the last two years. They are setting reduction goals to evaluate progress. One of the first steps in reduction is to use both sides of the paper in office use and printing. First, the staff is encouraged to use e-mail instead of paper memos, and not to print them. Next, one networked printer is dedicated for reusing paper already printed on one side. All the staff is responsible for saving single-sided paper in desk-side bins and loading the dedicated printer. This requires training to introduce staff to the process, and means staff must create new habits of intentionally printing from the appropriate printer. But such a simple arrangement can significantly reduce paper purchase and disposal—a money saver all around. These savings can help or completely cover the cost of paper with recycled content, if there is any additional cost, and you can bask in the synergy of reduced material needing recycling. Models for reductions in paper use can come from any sector: municipalities have tips and data online as do colleges and universities. In the case of Penn State, in one laboratory building, the staff committed to reducing paper use by a variety of measures—widening margins, using single spacing, double-sided printing, and reducing font size—they saved per capita paper costs of $25 per year even with 100 percent postconsumer recycled content.[2] You could choose any metric you want to measure the savings: gallons of water, kilowatt hours of electricity, acres of forest, tons of carbon emissions, and so on. The dollar and environmental savings in paper reduction can be significant.

What about nonpaper waste? Start with the low-hanging fruit here, too: banish plastic water bottles. Do you really have to sell them to your visitors and staff? Do the vending machines make that much money—if you factor in the energy to run them and the staff time to oversee them—do you also want to dispose of or recycle the bottles? Do you want to pick them up off the ground, out of the parking lot, and out from under seats in your orientation space? Would drinking fountains serve the same purpose? How do they fit into your energy and water efficiency plans?

Consider form and package. Buy in bulk; buy concentrated. Concentrated and bulk products can reduce the amount of packaging you purchase, use, and dispose of. They reduce the amount of packaging required to sell or send it to you, and therefore the waste in fuel for transport and materials for disposal. Be sure, however, to talk with the manufacturer about the concentrating process. You do not want the process to do more harm than good. If you do end up with plastic, choose types 1 and 2 because they are the most often accepted HDPE (high-density polyethylene) forms for recycling. Opt for compostable, reusable, or recyclable packaging—or no packaging at all. If you cannot eliminate packaging, look for ways to reduce it. Smaller, lighter packages use less energy for transportation.

You can ask your gift shop vendors to use biodegradable packing peanuts, or you can arrange to donate your peanuts to the local mail or package store for reuse. Vendors may be willing to forgo shrink-wrap or plastic bags if you ask them and work out a solution. Can you change your vending machines from beverages in plastic bottles to beverages in aluminum? Recycling aluminum can be profitable if you have a buyer in your area.

Anything in bulk reduces packaging consumption and waste disposal. You could start with a commitment to providing water in pitchers at your conferences and meetings. So at meetings, substitute iced tea or lemonade in pitchers instead of soda in cans; pour cream from carafes instead of providing individual plastic packages; and order lunches on platters instead of in carry boxes or plastic containers. It all reduces the environmental costs associated with producing and disposing of materials. In your café use condiment dispensers instead of packets; if you cannot commit to washing a full set of dishes, maybe you can at least wash silverware and reduce the plastic spoons, knives, and forks your guests use.

Reuse

Reuse what you have or what you collect from others. Remember, this is the whole environment we are protecting, not just your acre of it. We have already talked about the Museum of Fine Arts in Boston's shift to transport packaging as permanent storage packaging as reuse, and the exhibition design community is already tuned into trading exhibit furniture and casework among museums. Consider doing the same with all sorts of goods. Parents and artists throughout Boston know the Recycle Shop at the Boston Children's Museum is a treasure trove of industrial odds and ends, from game pieces to package trimmings, all perfect for at-home arts and crafts activities. The museum makes money on others' waste. Chesapeake Bay Maritime Museum (CBMM) sells tote bags made from old boat sails. They are handsome, durable, and reused material. ECHO sells tote bags, placemats, wallets, and purses made from its own reused museum exhibit banners. Now *that's* thinking.

Any frontline program staff knows the value of collecting resources for museum programs: toilet paper rolls, yogurt cups, cans, pie plates, cardboard boxes, fabric scraps—anything your staff and volunteers can get their hands on or vendors unwittingly provide. For KidsTown programs at the CBMM, at special events like Oysterfest, children make oyster creatures with oyster shells from area restaurants, decorate empty cans with adaptations of historic oyster labels, and make their own oyster plates from the historic images of the decorative platters for serving oysters on the half-shell. The staff and volunteers collected cans on-site and at home, and the staff used the backside of old event posters for cut-out oyster shapes children could color and glue on paper plates. Kids create oyster shell creatures by gluing on all sorts of cut-up, left-over decorations from evening events. The museum reduces waste and material purchases while creating an engaging public program. Of course, storing the materials takes space and organization, but it saves the staff time they would have spent to research, order, and process the goods, plus they saved the trash space and cost. Synergy.

Reusable tableware is often overlooked as a waste-reduction opportunity, but museums' cafés, special events, and on-site meetings produce a horrifying amount of plastic trash when they could use old-fashioned plates. The café at the Adirondack Museum went to reusable tableware once it became clear it was more efficient for staff to use a dishwasher for catering and in-house events. The synergy with the café enhanced the benefits. Shedd Aquarium café has shifted to cloth napkins and reusable tableware for all board, staff, and cultivation functions. It is a classier arrangement and environmentally appropriate. Your institution may want to require café and event caterers to shift to reusable goods only. Use your market muscle to offer exclusive rental access to those vendors who commit to using agreed-upon sustainable practices including reusing and recycling materials, and using sustainable sources. The Monterey Bay Aquarium's (MBAq) policy states, "The merchandise we carry and the guidelines we provide to vendors are powerful tools for affecting public perception and changing the buying practices of our suppliers. We use these to promote conservation awareness, and we share what we do with colleagues."

How to Recycle

Recycling comes in many forms: recycling by staff, visitors, and the community using municipal or private services; and selling recyclable materials or recycled goods on-site or through vendors. Increasingly museums are selling recycled goods, or those with recycled content, in our shops. The Adirondack Museum sells sweatshirts made from recycled cotton. But what about recycling materials used or generated on-site? The question is no longer whether or not to recycle, but how to make it work. A decision to recycle affects staff who process the materials, space use for storing the materials, vendor contracts for removing the materials, reductions in garbage hauling, and possible changes in costs for either garbage or recycling. It is not an isolated process. You will need to consider: How much of which recyclable materials do you generate? How much can you sell any of it for? How much processing and storing would it take to make it salable or removable to a recycling location?

Recycling involves a vendor who can process the materials off-site, and who usually comes to collect it from you. Sometimes they buy your material; often they just haul it for a cost, but often for less than the cost to haul garbage to the dump. Again, understanding the costs, components, and benefits of the process is important to making a decision. There are lots of questions: What are the barriers to recycling? Will the staff do it? What can you do to make it simple? What vendors and organizations can help you and in what ways? Is this a program for public education or benefit, or just an in-house program? What do you want to accomplish by recycling? Is it about cost, responsibility, or both? How does this fit with your overall sustainability policy: is it a priority or one of many components? How does this affect the triple bottom line?

Let's start with costs. They will certainly vary by state, region, and even locality. Recycling laws, municipal regulations, and vendor availability are key factors in how much recycling you can do. For some, it costs; for others, it is a break-even proposition; and for some, it pays (table 3.1). Nancy Hughes has been the Cleveland Metroparks Zoo's compost and recycling coordinator since 2003. In 1994 the zoo's Resource Management Committee—an early, early green team—began recycling. Composting was added in 1997 as the team worked with waste haulers to explore how to reduce their costs. Nancy's position is now full-time and permanent, and the (recycling) money's pretty good. Earned income from recycling has risen from

TABLE 3.1. Cleveland Metroparks Zoo Recycling Amounts

Recycling is one of the easiest ways for people to reduce their excessive use of natural resources. As part of our conservation mission, the zoo has developed an effective resource management program to recycle as many materials as possible. Yearly recycling totals are listed in the table.

Recyclable Material	2003	2004	2005	2006
Aluminum	665 pounds	1.16 tons	2.55 tons	2.30 tons
Appliances	8	13	17	17
Batteries (vehicle and other)	19	33	35 + 131*	34 + 182* + 116 rechargeable
Cardboard	n/a	23.71 tons	38.59 tons	41.06 tons
Cell phones*	n/a	n/a	322	816
Computer equipment**	n/a	n/a	107 pcs.	115 pcs.
Fluorescent lamps	2739**	1921**	1631	2008
Glass	1.78 tons	3.92 tons	7.62 tons	4.87 tons
Inkjet and toner cartridges*	n/a	160	456	889
Metals (copper, steel, iron, etc.)	8.93 tons	13.08 tons	14.00 tons	24.93 tons
Pallets	132	286	400 + 1.39 tons	240
Paper	13.59 tons	95.23 tons*	79.09 tons*	54.56 tons*
Phonebooks*	24.65 tons	18.63 tons	14.89 tons	15.61 tons
Plastic containers	1.25 tons	2.18 tons	1300 pounds + 18 8-yd. containers	23 8-yd. containers
Plastic shrink wrap and signs	n/a	n/a	4 bins	5 bins
Tires	293	293	357	335
Vehicle waste (antifreeze, oil, solvents, oil filters)	479 gals.	830 gals.	66 gals.	663 gals.
Recycling Receipts	**$973.09**	**$5,014.31**	**$7,463.27**	**$11,089.10**

*Includes public participation.
**Includes Metroparks Reservations.
Public recycling collection sites are provided at all zoo picnic areas and placed throughout the zoo to collect plastic and glass bottles and aluminum waste generated by our visitors. Concession vendors are required to participate in recycling efforts at all concessions and catered events. All cardboard cartons are added to the recycling waste stream.
Source: Tom O'Konowitz

$963 in 2003 when she arrived, to over $11,000 part-way through 2007. Money raised through the paper recycling program more than covered the cost of the $10,500 cardboard baler the zoo purchased to package its recyclable cardboard for sale to a waste contractor. The baler paid for itself within the year. Will you have the same results compared to these high-volume cases? Not necessarily, but it is worth doing your research to find out what the payback could be if you capitalized on the opportunity.

Corrugated cardboard is often the easiest salable recycling. Some vendors buy clean, dry boxes as is, but if you have the volume and can work up to owning a baling machine like Shedd (reconditioned balers can cost as little as $3,500), you can sell your corrugated cardboard for anywhere from $20 to $40 a ton. The cash value is greater, though, because you do not also have to pay to haul it. If you do not generate enough on your own, perhaps together the area museums can buy a baler and recycle and sell their cardboard.

Recycling aluminum cans is an income generator, especially if you have a food service program. Vendors buy aluminum to remake into all sorts of items. Recycled aluminum reduces energy use by 90 to 95 percent. It is cheaper to recycle than to produce. You could realize from $350 to nearly $1,000 per ton, depending upon the area markets. Zoo Atlanta's website offers compelling statistics to encourage aluminum recycling:

❖ Recycling one aluminum can or one glass container saves enough energy to keep a 100-watt bulb burning for almost four hours or to run your television for three hours.

❖ In 2006, 54 billion cans were recycled, saving energy equivalent to 15 million barrels of crude oil—America's entire gas consumption for one day.

❖ Aluminum is the most abundant metal on earth. It is a durable and sustainable metal: two-thirds of the aluminum ever produced is still in use today.

❖ A used aluminum can is recycled and back on the grocery shelf as a new can, in as little as sixty days.

Do your café or gift shop items arrive on pallets? You can often sell them for $1.00 to $1.50 each. If you cannot find a buyer, look for a nearby manufacturer to collect them and reuse them for their shipping needs. For both cardboard and pallets, and for many other recycling activities, the staff costs for breaking down, sorting, or baling are similar to traditional garbage sorting requirements. Is it really any harder to pitch the boxes into a baler or to stack the pallets for pickup? Some recycling activities, however, will be more time consuming than traditional disposal. Either way, you will have to calculate return on investment according to your institutional policy and goals.

If you are engaged in construction, renovations, or exhibition reinstallations, sort your construction waste. If you have a contractor, make it a part of the expected services. Whether they do it or you do it, use a source like "A Contractor's Waste Management Guide" put out by the Hawaiian government with descriptions for types of waste to separate, and the weight and value of the material. Resources like this one will help you rethink everything you throw in the dumpster on demolition day.

Recycling construction waste and hazardous materials are special situations because of the nature of the materials and the legal requirements. EPA requirements for hazardous materials like fluorescent lightbulbs mean staff must repackage spent bulbs in original packaging materials and pay to have a vendor remove them. However, if you are in King County in Washington state, you are eligible for reimbursement of 50 percent of the cost of recycling those lamps and ballasts, up to $500 per site. Do your research and find out what you can sell your materials for. You won't know if you don't ask.

How do you find out? See what is online. Your state's recycling program is a good start. The EPA site has a clickable map for locating recycling resources in your area. The Association of Vermont Recyclers posts a School Waste Reduction Guide online with tips on doing a waste audit or assessment, and forms to help. There are similar sites at least for Arizona, California, Ohio, Illinois, New York and Pennsylvania, the Northeast, New Zealand, and Canada. If you do not like the material on your state's site, use another's. Many states have composting associations or councils with applicable advice.

Each museum will have different tonnage results, of course. Your institution may not reach a critical mass that creates this payback either in sold goods or reduced hauling costs. You may not be in an area where vendors buy recyclable materials. If financial viability is the main criterion, consider creating a collaborative to reach the totals you need. It may mean combining waste to attract a buyer or to reach a critical mass that covers hauling costs.

You can also ask the public to help. At The Discovery Museums in Acton, Massachusetts, they have an Abitibi Paper Retriever program where the public contributes grocery bags of recyclable paper. It promotes recycling at the museums and in the community. The museums barely reach the minimum one-ton-per-month amount, in the early stages of the program, but with their frequent-flier card granting free admission after twelve bags, the program will develop a following. One young visitor brought all twelve bags in one visit because she wanted her free admission. The public helps out at the Cleveland Metroparks Zoo, too. The zoo's website promotes its on-site public paper, cell phone, and toner recycling centers at the zoo. The materials are sold to recycling vendors and the proceeds directed to the recycling, composting, and conservation efforts of the museum. That is a double benefit: public service and education, with a financial benefit for the zoo.

These single-item or limited-item recycling programs for cell phones, ink cartridges, juice packets, plastic bottles, batteries, and other items provide materials for reuse by special purpose vendors with some payback. Some of these vendors may have limited capacity for recycling, and some may occasionally limit or discontinue programs. Beware that there may be interruptions in a carefully cultivated habit that may complicate your waste stream management process. So just as you source products carefully, source your recycling vendors with considerations for longer-term relationships.

Remember, you can get the vendor to assess your needs and quote a price for you to use in decision making. You may even be able to put the hauling and recycling contracts out to bid. And you can band together with your neighbors, museums, and others, to create a supply and demand situation to your benefit.

Recycling Success

It is worth being realistic about the staff implications of a recycling program. Educate staff so they can recycle appropriately by sorting materials carefully and correctly, and provide consistent encouragement and support to keep recycling an important part of regular duties, not orphaned as afterthoughts or time-available work. Keeping everyone educated on the importance and the process is time consuming, especially with occasional workers, seasonals, and interns, and turnover in volunteers and staff. Organizations can incorporate training into regular orientations or add it to the series of sessions during the year. "You can't increase participation without education," says Nancy Hughes.

Making it easy is something Miriam Kessler promoted at the New York Hall of Science. Their green team was bringing back paper recycling in the offices. The green team investigated the problems holding back museum staff from recycling their used copy paper, cardboard, and catalogs, and then met with the vice president of facilities and security to figure out what steps to take to make recycling paper easy and convenient for facilities staff to process and all museum staff to initiate. The solution was enough office- and cubicle-friendly recycling bins for everyone and then to deliver the bins during an all-staff meeting along with a recycling demonstration; yes, demonstration. Sometimes that is what it takes to spread an idea.

At ECHO, in true science center-educator form, they evaluated the current office recycling program to determine what worked and what did not; then they refined it. They observed where the recyclable materials were most likely to be used (and therefore recycled), where there was space for recycling bins, and what cues staff needed to identify material-bin matches. The blue bins at desks have a paper tray over them to encourage staff to consider if the paper has been used on both sides and should be recycled; one-sided printed pages should be kept for use in the copier that prints on used paper for in-house, nonconfidential uses. The bins for cans, bottles, and so on are located in a central hallway near the exit and near the employee lounge (there is also one in the café, but that requires visitor training, too). The bins all have clip art images that Silverman has prototyped to test their effectiveness. It takes just a few minutes to find and print a symbol, and tape it to two or three test bins. As prototyping continues, the team has heard that clear recycling bins dramatically increase recycling accuracy. (Think how much more effective it is to have a clear donation box with money in it than a donation box that you cannot see into.) Silverman keeps an eye on bin use and accuracy of the recycling—a casual waste audit—and can judge if the symbol is or is not more effective. In the meantime the team is developing a simple training that can be tacked onto a staff meeting or new employee orientation. Facts and figures can help. The Union of Concerned Scientists' online Great Green Web Game (accessed November 2007) has some goodies: office paper is 10 percent of most municipalities' waste, and the largest contributor.

When you have a staff of over five or so, or working different shifts, group training is important for sharing messages and protocols. ECHO's staff of twenty-five is dispersed in three types of areas and some groups mix less with others. Group training shares the recycling ethos and information. The green team uses behind-the-scenes work to test change before putting it in the public eye. Silverman says, "the idea is that staff needs to really internalize any behavioral changes before ... engaging the guest in behavior changes." And since new green procedures and protocols may require staff to change their daily work procedures and communication with guests, it makes sense to practice before preaching.

Observations and training discussions might highlight some barriers to the reduce-reuse-recycle process. Space limitations might make it difficult to place receptacles conveniently. There may be no room for recycle bins at each desk, or the only can recycling bin may be in the main hall and there is no space in the corridor or staff lunch room. Would adding a divider to an existing bin do the trick? Is it worth the $80 to buy an aluminum can crusher/container (it looks like a garbage can and holds 400 cans)? Can staff and volunteers lift and manage the bags, containers, or bales of materials that you use for recycling? If not, can you reengineer the process to make it comfortable enough that anyone can happily comply? Just making it possible is never good enough. Making the process easy increases participation.

Consider outside sources for training and collaborative efforts. At larger institutions specialized staff may hold professional memberships and participate in training that exposes them to new vendors and best practices. Hughes attends conferences in Ohio of the Association of Ohio Recyclers, National Recycling Coalition, U.S. Composting Council, and the Ohio Composting Association. Your municipality may offer recycling workshops and consortium benefits. The Chesapeake Gateways Network offered a free Greening Your Gateway symposium to consortium members and sent home free composting bins with all the participants. Letting your community leaders know what you are doing may bring you allies. They may be interested in making changes or expanding services but are unsure of participation. If they know you are interested and supportive, they may be motivated to move forward with their own recycling efforts.

It all comes down to what you want to accomplish with recycling. Is it about no cost, low cost, profit, or simply because it is the right thing to do? Is it a public program, so you provide educational materials at the recycle bins? Is it a community contribution, so you should collaborate with others or provide a community recycling opportunity? Is it about the triple bottom line?

What you do will change over time. Many museums started their sustainability programs with that one staff member who took home the recyclables because the museum did not have a program. Sometimes that home-based approach continues even when a hauler is found, since at a cost of $100 per month, the staff chooses to save it for program expenses. Maybe when the costs drop to $50, the amount of recyclables grows, or the institutional policy expands, the decision will change; maybe it will not. Each museum makes its own decisions. Policies and information ease the process and produce defensible results.

At the moment, few of us can have a zero-waste museum. While we are working toward it, we still have garbage to get rid of. At ECHO, they have thought about it. They use completely biodegradable and compostable garbage bags, which are stable until used (yet last two weeks curbside before beginning to break down) and contain no petroleum. So at least the bag the garbage is in does not add to the landfill.

There are similar biodegradable bags for dog waste. If your open space is dog accessible, consider strategically placed dispensers with these. Cleaning up dog waste is considerate of other walkers and reduces fecal matter in storm water runoff by diverting it appropriately to a landfill where it should be contained and managed more appropriately. At least the poop bag is not petroleum-based plastic.

Composting

Composting is reducing and recycling combined. (We will get to composting toilets later on.) It reduces landfill waste by recycling organic material, and that waste diversion is its own huge environmental saving. As the plastics and green industries expand, the variety of compostable alternatives for packaging is expanding, but do read the fine print. Composting occurs under special conditions of moisture and temperature that do not usually exist in a landfill. So if your compostable plastic ends up in the garbage, it is not guaranteed to compost at the dump.

You can have compostable materials hauled to a composting center as Shedd does, or you can compost onsite. Pittsburgh Children's Museum uses worm bins for composting café materials; so does OMSI (figure 3.2). They felt that if they were encouraging visitors to use them at home, they should be using them at the museum. ZooDoo, ZooPoo, and other variations on the popular theme of composting zoo manure have been around for awhile. The Cleveland Metroparks Zoo, as well as others, uses much of the composted gardening leftovers, manure, hay, straw, wood shavings, and wood chips on the gardens throughout its 168 acres, but also sells its ZooPoo Compost twice yearly. For the last four years the zoo has sold out of its limited quantities. The public can make advance purchases online and collect it on one of two pickup days. The cost is $3 for a five-gallon bucket or $10 for a thirty-two-gallon can, and $35 for a cubic yard. Newer and smaller zoos may use the compost on-site to reduce purchases of plant food, fertilizer, and mulch, and they can give it to staff and volunteers as a benefit.

Green Products and Sourcing

Sourcing products means finding sources that sell or provide green materials, products, and services, and it means examining the materials, products, and services to determine the true extent and nature of green practice. Sourcing applies to your café, shop, events, offices, exhibits, printers, promotions—everything.

For existing products you want to know the environmental impact of where the ingredients come from and how they were collected. Ask how they were combined to produce the product you are considering, how it gets to you, and how it affects the environment when you use it. With all that information you can choose which materials, products, and services provide the

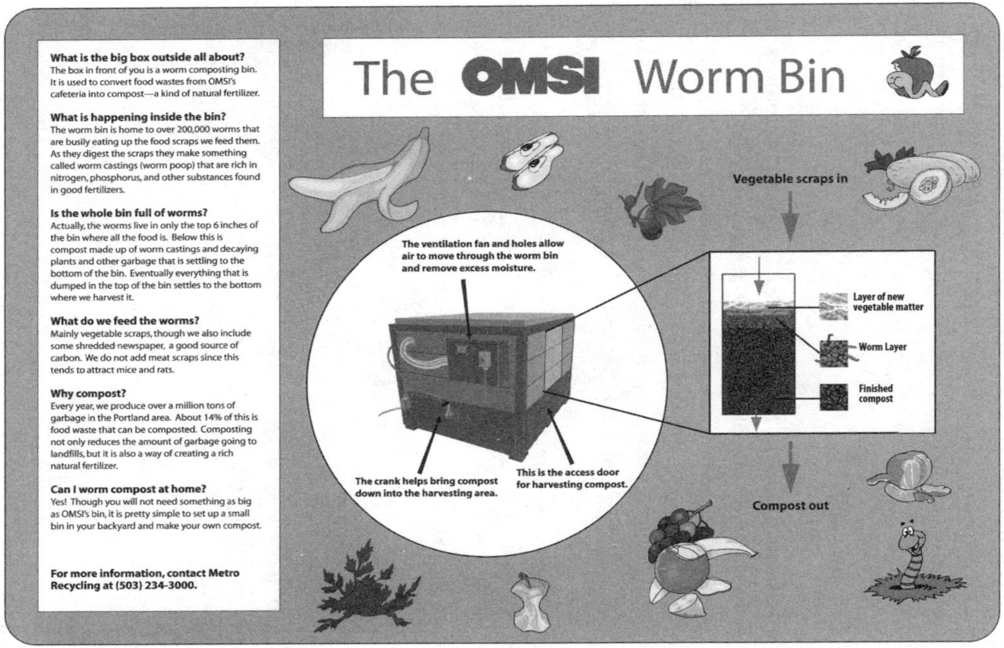

FIGURE 3.2. Sustainable actions are educational opportunities. The Oregon Museum of Science and Industry has a cross-functional green team dedicated to advancing sustainability and to coordinating and communicating those efforts among 300 staff and a multitude of volunteers. When the museum set about measuring and then reducing their waste stream, they realized food waste from their café operations represented a significant percentage of volume and weight in their dumpster. To reduce the café's impact on their waste stream, the museum started a vermicomposting operation and, in line with their commitment to turn every sustainable action into an educational opportunity, they devised interpretive signage to explain how their worm bin works. Courtesy OMSI

The **OMSI** Worm Bin

Vegetable scraps in

Layer of new vegetable matter

Worm Layer

Finished compost

Compost out

The ventilation fan and holes allow air to move through the worm bin and remove excess moisture.

This is the access door for harvesting compost.

The crank helps bring compost down into the harvesting area.

What is the big box outside all about?
The box in front of you is a worm composting bin. It is used to convert food wastes from OMSI's cafeteria into compost—a kind of natural fertilizer.

What is happening inside the bin?
The worm bin is home to over 200,000 worms that are busily eating up the food scraps we feed them. As they digest the scraps they make something called worm castings (worm poop) that are rich in nitrogen, phosphorus, and other substances found in good fertilizers.

Is the whole bin full of worms?
Actually, the worms live in only the top 6 inches of the bin where all the food is. Below this is compost made up of worm castings and decaying plants and other garbage that is settling to the bottom of the bin. Eventually everything that is dumped in the top of the bin settles to the bottom where we harvest it.

What do we feed the worms?
Mainly vegetable scraps, though we also include some shredded newspaper, a good source of carbon. We do not add meat scraps since this tends to attract mice and rats.

Why compost?
Every year, we produce over a million tons of garbage in the Portland area. About 14% of this is food waste that can be composted. Composting not only reduces the amount of garbage going to landfills, but it is also a way of creating a rich natural fertilizer.

Can I worm compost at home?
Yes! Though you will not need something as big as OMSI's bin, it is pretty simple to set up a small bin in your backyard and make your own compost.

For more information, contact Metro Recycling at (503) 234-3000.

least impact and satisfy your needs. You may find yourself rethinking your needs, or the way you use materials, and rethinking your vendors. Creating policy on sourcing products will help your museum consistently consider the environment.

For example, the Museum Store Association (MSA) board of directors has adopted an ethics policy addressing the sale of materials from endangered species. It is illegal to sell materials incorporating ivory from Asian and African elephants. For walrus ivory, only that certified as Native Alaskan Handicraft is acceptable. The National Marine Fisheries Service governs the use of material from sperm, blue, bowhead, finback, gray, right, and Sei whales. Material certified in the United States before December 28, 1973, is acceptable; all else is not. Why is this so important that it is part of an ethics statement? Because these items are part of natural heritage or threatened or endangered species.

The MBAq's policy says,

> We sell no products produced from living creatures if those products send an inappropriate message about the conservation of wildlife and ecosystems. We will not do business with vendors that manufacture, distribute or sell such products to other customers. We require direct or written documentation from our business partners and vendors regarding origin of living materials used in their products.

Ignorance is no excuse for selling ivory or whale products. At the moment it *is* an excuse for selling products made from unsustainable sources or with unsustainable methods. If you sell wood products, furniture for example, does your vender require the wood to come from responsibly managed forests?

The MSA policy states,

> It is the obligation of the seller to know and to satisfy the requirements of all laws protecting a particular species, whether plant or wildlife, whose parts or products are intended for sale through the MSA. Sellers should be prepared to provide any and all documentation and certificates of exemption as required by the Convention on International trade in Endangered Species (CITES), the Endangered Species Act (ESA) or state law.

While you are talking with the vendor about sources, remember they are interested in serving you and in providing the materials you want. Discuss what green products they offer or would be willing to offer. They may tell you of practices they use that you did not realize. The UC Davis Design Museum outsources some of its printed needs to a specifically green vendor: they use soy- and vegetable-based inks and buy carbon offsets for shipping, but they also keep all transactions paper-free and online for proofing and paying.

For Offices

It is very easy to locate green office supplies and cleaning materials online. The office can use recycled-content copier paper, sticky notes, notepads, easel pads, and stationery. Consider the recycled content of bathroom paper and source green cleaning materials. The best companies will send it to you packaged in recyclable materials. Many organizations require all the purchasing to go through one staff member, which is a great way to ensure green selections. Setting policy for the buyer will help, too. Do you want to require your paper to have 100 percent postconsumer recycled content, and all other materials to be 100 percent recyclable? At least require your items to be made without bleaching.

Tanya Salvey, administrative assistant for Shedd's Conservation, Marine Mammals, and Animal Health departments, has worked with Chicago's Warehouse Direct to create a green contracted items list. The company provides the products at lower cost because the aquarium and others in Chicago's Green Museum Consortium guarantee purchases of the items. Shedd even sends over its own reused cardboard boxes for pickup to reduce packaging (there is no extra fuel use because the Warehouse truck would go back and forth anyway). Not every product is going to be green, but Salvey encourages other staff to select green items by highlighting them on the preprinted order sheets she provides.

Give yourself credit for what you already do—and then keep doing it. Continue to reuse file folders, rewritable CDs, and intraoffice memo envelopes (where you cross out your name at the bottom of the list and add the next as you reroute it). One museum standby has long been sustainable: compact storage. For decades museums have been using compact, mobile storage and shelving units. Compact storage reduces energy demands for controlling larger spaces and eliminates or delays the need to build or lease additional storage space—decidedly ungreen behavior.

You might have to get more inventive with special products. At ECHO the entire staff knew they needed more visitor seating distributed through exhibits and waiting areas. Educators and others looked at a variety of options but found no "fit." The need went unaddressed longer than anyone wanted, simply because they could not find a solution that suited the mission and esthetic of the institution. Then they found a local woodworker who uses reclaimed lumber. Together, ECHO staff and the local crafter designed recycled red oak benches that are unique, beautiful, earth friendly, and a pleasure to sit on. Julie Silverman points out that patience is often important for finding a satisfying solution. The result supported their institution mantra of "a healthier place to live"; it just was not obvious early on.

At Shedd, the sea otters gobble tons of shrimp every year, but the harvesting practices for imported wild-caught shrimp can cause serious habitat damage, and large amounts of wildlife are regularly caught in trawling nets for shrimp. Imported shrimp often comes with a lower price tag, an important attribute when you have nearly 26,000 animals to feed. Shedd did not want their otters' diet to contribute to the environmental issues associated with imported shrimp, so they turned to Desert Sweet Shrimp, a small sustainable farm in Arizona. The farm uses fresh water pumped from underground to the ponds for growing the shrimp, and then uses it, with a few more nutrients from the shrimp, to irrigate nearby fields. The natural sunlight warms the water and encourages faster growth for larger shrimp. But those are not the reasons that make this sustainable from Shedd's point of view. The original need for 12,000 pounds of shrimp each year has been reduced to 7,000 pounds, thanks to the quality and efficient packaging of the product, bringing Shedd significant savings on their annual feed bill. As for the otters, the shrimp immediately won over their finicky palates, making their trainers happy, too.

Green Food Service and Systems

Food sourcing and waste management are key issues for food services associated with museums. When the New York Hall of Science began exploring green behaviors, it worked on the inside and the outside. In partnership with Community Markets, it hosts four farmers in a market at the front door of the museum in Queens. The goal is "to support local agriculture, strengthen local communities, and make fresh produce available to neighborhoods with limited access." The education department creates Kitchen Botany handouts and programs that identify and explain types of fruits and vegetables, plant origins and adaptations, the importance of scientific names of plants, and, of course, how to eat them. "Reducing the miles your food travels by buying locally grown food helps preserve fossil fuels, which is one step towards stemming global warming," said Hall president and CEO Marilyn Hoyt. "We are happy to offer the community and our visitors terrific fresh produce and hands-on learning in agriculture and fresh foods."

What about the food you serve in your café or dining facility? We learned long ago when our museum shops became teaching resources that every aspect of the museum is a teaching opportunity and an exhibit. That extends to the food service.

Phipps has Get Green symbols throughout the facility as cues for green messaging: that means in the bathrooms, throughout the exhibits, and in the café. The interpretive panels for sustainability are mixed with the garden interpretation signs. This tells the visitors that the sustainability message is on par with the exhibit message. In the café, Phipps provides and highlights local and organic produce and beverages. Reclaiming regional fare is an important sustainability opportunity and can be part of your educational message. On the wall menus, magnetized symbols indicate locally grown or mostly organic food. The boards list local farm suppliers, identifies the coffee as shade grown, explains that the beer is regional, and point out that Phipps grows its own herbs. Signage explains that at least 50 percent of the paper in the coffee cups is recycled material, and the napkins are 100 percent recycled. Plastic cups are made from corn.[3] They use real utensils instead of plastic disposable ones. Of course, they ask visitors to recycle glass and plastic bottles. Signs over the receptacles say "Want to help?" and direct visitors to Phipps' website for more ideas on recycling and living sustainably.

At ECHO, they have transformed the café into an interactive exhibit, the Green Café, where food choice and waste management (recycling and composting) are the activities. The main messages are environmental solid waste management practices of reduce, reuse, recycle, and composting; choose your food wisely; consider buying local, Vermont fresh, seasonal, nutritious, and delicious; fair-trade foods; think about community connections; and energy efficiency and green construction. Silverman says, "It's all about choices." She says they are exploring messages and games placed on tables and trays that encourage people: "Play with your food!" or "Sort your lunch into groups—things that can be composted, things that are made of plastic," and so on. Supporting information explains why buying local is a good economic and healthy choice. The new recycling and composting center demonstrates what and how to recycle and compost. Visitors consider the choices each can make about reducing waste: use a travel mug or disposable cups; and use a lunch bag or box, or disposable prepacked lunches.

At Shedd the staff handles recycling, and Paganis has sophisticated waste management systems in place. What began with her as the garbage lady hauling home compost is now integrated through the aquarium's dining room and cafeteria. The staff handles the food service recycling and composting, not the public. That is because the staff is better at it. Items are separated into clear compostable bags. Shedd recycles frying oil, composts vegetable waste, bales cardboard for recycling, uses bulk purchasing to reduce trash, recycles wine corks for reusing as flooring, and has searched out new types of recyclable packaging. The staff plans ahead by defrosting meat in the refrigerator for three days, instead of at the last minute with running cold water. Paganis buys bulk sugar and creamer and offers these and condiments in dispensers instead of providing individual packets. The high-use cafeteria tables have butcher paper over cloth to reduce the amount of linen washing.

MBAq has led the way in sustainable choices for its restaurants and in encouraging the public to make sustainable choices in any restaurant they visit. Their Seafood Watch webpage includes "Which Seafood to Buy and Why," "Your Choices Matter," and "What Can You Do?" With increasing demand for seafood, aquaculture is growing, but it has advantages and disadvantages. The website has great information for an active learner, and to extend the reach they promote their Seafood Watch program for recommending what seafood to choose and avoid, and why. Visitors can print and carry pocket-sized versions of MBAq's regional seafood and national guides.

The New England Aquarium (NEAq) suggests website visitors connect to the MBAq's seafoodwatch.org site, and oceansalive.org or NEAq's Fish of the Month site online. The web page recommends sustainable seafood choices by highlighting a fish each month, with recipes as well as information on fishing and farming practices, and conservation notes. NEAq also offers a Celebrate Seafood Dinner Series. This "fine dining experience for ocean and seafood lovers alike" is a mix of food education, a three-course meal with wine, expert cooking demonstrations, and aquarium researchers' presentations. Paying guests sample and learn about smart seafood choices they can prepare for themselves at home. All the seafood is "caught or farmed in environmentally responsible ways."

The California Academy of Sciences had six bidders for its contract to provide food service in its new café. Each embraced the requirement to provide a positive financial return and programmatic support that would create a seamless message of sustainability from exhibition areas to the eating area. Each promised to demonstrate and interpret sustainable practices by explaining and labeling products and processes for the visitors.[4]

As in the sourcing discussion above, consider the environmental impact of products used in your café. Local and organic foods are good. Shade-grown coffee is good because it is produced without clear-cutting rainforest, our single greatest terrestrial source of the oxygen we breathe, and home to two-thirds of all the living species on the planet. Plastics made from corn are renewable, but the jury is out on the total environmental impact of corn plastic. It is compostable, but only at 150 degrees with 90 percent humidity. That works if you have a controlled compost program. At least it is also ideal for composting your vegetable waste. The food service industry has jumped into green in a big way. There are vendors (some with hundreds of national accounts at corporations, colleges, museums, and national parks) dedicated integrating environmentally sustainable practices into their operations.[5]

This kind of market muscle is driving the development of new products and approaches. Still, the old reduce, reuse, recycle mantra applies. Reduce waste by using dishes, cutlery, glasses, and porcelain coffee cups and washing them in dishwashers, if you are able; if not, check online to see what the latest developments are in recycled, tree-free, biodegradable, and chlorine-free paper products.[6] There are recycling programs for waste oils, fats, and grease. Some entrepreneurs are turning these by-products into biodiesel and one job training program for homeless people in New York City offers an on-demand pickup service.[7] As always, connecting these activities to your educational mission through signage and other means is a big plus.

Green Cleaning and Maintenance

Thinking outside traditional custodial methods and working together on collaborative solutions is critical to long-term results. Colonial Williamsburg Foundation's (CWF) conservator of exhibits, Patty Silence, worked with the custodians at the Dewitt Wallace Decorative Arts Museum and the new Abby Aldrich Rockefeller Folk Art Museum (AARFAM) on floor cleaning protocols to reduce airborne particulates and the need for cleaning fluids and refinishing agents. The custodians agree that more frequent floor dusting with microfiber dust mops (larger ones in the morning for fewer passes, smaller ones during open hours so as not to interfere with visitors) would also reduce the need for full-floor refinishing by controlling damaging grit. This lengthens the life of the floor and reduces the amount of time the museums are closed for floor work. It also reduces the time and energy required for contractors to refinish floors.

Never underestimate the power of walkoff mats or entryway grates. Whether outside or inside your doors, mats and grates trap grit, moisture, and mess before people and materials get too far into your building. This focuses your cleaning efforts on the entryway areas and not throughout the halls and rooms. It is far easier to clean a portable mat than to deep-clean permanent carpet. It is greener to clean or replace one mat than much larger areas of carpet and floor. Remember that promptly sweeping exterior walkways will contain the leaves, water, and deicing mess from entering the building, too. By keeping it all cleaner you reduce the chemical use for indoor cleaning, as well. You probably purchase cleaning fluids in bulk or concentrated amounts. Careful mixing is important to avoid overuse of chemicals from using too much cleaner, or recleaning of areas from using too little cleaner. Many vendors provide mechanical devices to ensure proper dilution ratios.

Remember the story of the Disney Go Green Campaign by the Center for Health, Environment and Justice? Switch to cleaning products that do not adversely affect the cleaning staff who use them and the people (staff and guests) who occupy the spaces where they are used. One children's museum has their buildings on regular cleaning rotation whereby each building is closed to the public and extensive cleaning takes place. That is good since all the hands-on exhibits have just that—grime and bacteria left behind by hands. Unfortunately the museum uses cleaning products that continue to off-gas well after the cleaning day is over and the building is reopened to guests. Those guests are school-aged children who are cavorting on the floor (a good thing) but up-close and personal with the same carpet just cleaned with toxic chemicals (not good).

Indoor air quality is important to health, productivity, and learning. Poor indoor air quality is also connected to skyrocketing rates of asthma. Your green operational plan should include recommendations about museum cleaning and maintenance procedures to minimize toxins and asthma triggers (a particular issue with the vulnerable school-age population). Segregate sources of pollutants (cleaning products, chemicals, etc.) and make a separate ventilated space for printers and copiers. Telling the story about those choices helps visitors to understand how they can make positive changes in their own homes. We have learned that increasingly school nurses are accompanying students on field trips due to the spike in asthma and upper respiratory illnesses. There is even discussion that field trips are being phased out as school districts reexamine their liability should emergencies occur. Having green cleaning and maintenance procedures that are posted and interpreted instills trust in the museum as an institution that cares for its visitors.

Green Exhibitions and Materials

Children's museums were early adopters of green. It grew out of concern for the health of their visitors—children who crawl over, climb through, handle, and mouth every inch of their carpets, structures, and other exhibition materials. In its 2004 expansion project the Children's Museum of Pittsburgh used only adhesives, sealants, paints, carpets, and composite wood that are certified formaldehyde free with near-zero off-gassing. The addition and other site improvements used renewable, reused, and recycled building materials so the whole place is an exhibition on green. This is only one of the many factors that won the building its 2006 designation as a LEED Silver building.[8]

The Madison Children's Museum is also known for its green materials and exhibitions recommendations. Finding nontoxic materials was a challenge, but they created their first green exhibition, traveled it for five years and have kept up that work ever since. Their experiences, and those of other museums, are presented as case studies on their website. It has excellent information for all your green exhibition planning, not just children's exhibitions.[9] In general they have found that green material durability is impressive, often outlasting traditional exhibit materials. The payback is longevity as well as indoor air quality and visitor health and safety.

At the University of California, Davis, Tim McNeil, director of the Design Museum, teaches exhibition design. He and his students are exploring green exhibit design. He feels that designers are very proactive with ways to be green in exhibit and signage materials, and that his students—your future exhibition designers and fabricators—are very savvy in green issues. "They want to be involved and want to do something," he says. "There's so much information out there that it's impossible to keep up." But in his classes and their exhibits they continue to pursue new possibilities. The UC Davis Design Museum has a staff of three and a collection of 5,000 objects, so they are a great site for experimenting with ways that small museums can become green.

First off, he recommends zero-volatile organic compound (VOC) paints and sealers. With three or four product lines currently and more coming online at a rapid pace, there is no excuse not to use them in exhibition and building finishes. At the Design Museum they are exploring and testing which paints are most appropriate for museum use. "Think of it," he says. "We paint walls for every exhibit. That's a lot of paint. We use low- and zero-VOC paint for our art, as a conservation principle; don't people deserve it as well?" And if we want to create a healthy environment for our visitors, too, not just our objects, then zero VOC is critical. He and his students are also testing the idea of only repainting the "area of vision" for the visitor—that space where the label or backdrop is critical, not the whole wall. The design focuses the visitors' gaze and interest, and the bonus is conservation of materials, time, and money in overall exhibition installation.

What about labels and exhibition graphics? The solvents in ink, the toxic manufacture of vinyl—all bad stuff. And those exhibition banners have a short life. Either we find ways to reuse or recycle them, or we find less environmentally damaging materials and processes for creating them. ECHO has the banners remade into bags and totes to sell. The Design Museum is currently using a nontoxic alternative PVC banner material that is also landfill degradable. McNeil also works with printers who use a range of inks called "eco-solvent" instead of the traditional ones that evaporate and release

VOCs while leaving an ink residue on your sign or banner. Legislation in some places, and common sense in many places, has led the print and sign industries to begin developing more eco-solvent inks and printers. Ask for them in your exhibit design and outdoor banners, and for exhibition "collateral" (press kits, catalogs, handouts). McNeil points out that large-format, short-run inkjet graphics should use eco-solvent inks (low solvent and petroleum content), and offset lithography collateral should use vegetable-based inks (soy) and postconsumer recycled content papers.

McNeil and his students have experimented with other materials as well. Consider wheatboard, a particle board made from compressed wheat stalks, a by-product from agriculture that was formerly burned. You can use it as an exhibit panel, repurpose it as a partition wall, repaint it, or recycle it since it is a natural, rapidly renewable material. Using cradle-to-cradle concepts of materials born from recycled materials that can then be recycled at the end of their life means that the 4 by 8 panel in your exhibit has a long first life with a good afterlife.[10] This sort of reuse concept is good for anyone, but particularly helpful to the most cost-conscious museums of any size. Planning to reuse components or repurpose materials for future exhibitions extends the value and enhances sustainability, too. Savvy exhibit design firms are offering modular exhibit furniture with interchangeable components (bases and vitrines) and reusable components (walls, tables, platforms, and play areas). This capitalizes on the skills we have developed for creating the components of traveling exhibits; only in this case the exhibit remains in place but changes appearance.

As with new buildings and renovations, green exhibition design starts with integrated design. If the fabricator is involved in exhibition development and green goals are expressed by the team before fabrication, we know you get a better result. For example, with the preparatory department onboard with sustainable practices, it is far easier to plan for renewable and reusable materials, low-VOC choices, and waste reduction in exhibits. Large museums have the larger volume larger exhibition spaces, therefore more material in them, and probably more frequent turnarounds of perhaps three to four months, which produces more exhibition waste. Many recognize the waste and are just coming to grips with how to manage it. They rightfully look at it as construction waste, not regular, daily museum waste. Still, separating the materials for recycling or reuse is critical. The Getty Center has a system whereby the hauler provides a separate dumpster for all exhibition construction waste. The nonsegregated material is hauled to a sorting center and the center receives credits for dollars off the $104 hauling fee. It is often a neutral cost for the construction waste dumpster, and a decrease in cost for total waste disposal. The material does not go to a landfill, is recycled for other uses, and is not part of the tonnage The Getty Center pays to haul away.

For those whose haulers require a segregated waste stream, once the exhibition staff or contractors are trained in the separation requirements, and the museum has a system for separating and hauling the materials, the process becomes green business as usual. So if you are using a contractor, include the separation process and the hauling and recycling as part of the RFP. Make it a criterion for exhibition development and construction at your museum. That would be a natural outgrowth of your exhibitions policy and your green policies.

Of course, you do not have to demolish all your exhibit materials. What you do not reuse might be reusable for another institution. McNeil points out that the manufacture of acrylic plastic sheet involves highly toxic substances and the material cannot be easily recycled, yet many of us use it regularly for vitrines. Trading materials among museums is an excellent way to reduce the waste stream, reuse materials, and save money. The Carlisle (Massachusetts) Historical Society benefits from hand-me-downs from the Bostonian Society, the Concord Museum, and the Museum of Our National Heritage. Surely others in your community would benefit from a freecycle-style program. Tempered glass is an alternative to acrylic that is recyclable and less prone to cracking and scratches than is acrylic. It costs more, but again there is good value in longevity and environmental benefit.

Green Exhibitions and Energy

There is significant synergy between exhibits and energy conservation. Designers and fabricators, if they are in on the project early, can help the entire design team grapple with lighting issues that address object conservation, visitor experience, and energy efficiency. Remember, cooler lights reduce your cooling bills. How do you keep them cool? Keep them off more, and use compact fluorescents (CFLs), LED lighting, or metal halides when you can. The use of LEDs in museum case lighting is improving and expanding.[11] McNeil says LEDs now deliver adequate cooler temperature, and lumens with the benefits of long life with a fraction of the energy use; though he points out that successful track lighting LED systems will take time.

Occupancy sensors keep the lights off when the public is not in the exhibit. This reduces light exposure for the object, and heat and energy loads for the building, but promises your visitor on-demand lighting. Reducing the heating load from the lights means your air conditioning system does not have to work as hard to cool the building. We have said before that energy efficiency is by far the greatest opportunity for costs savings and environmental benefit, so make it a priority to reexamine exhibit lighting. Twenty years ago CWF had some visitor-activated lights in its textile exhibition at its then-new Dewitt Wallace Decorative Arts Gallery. Now the textile and paper galleries in the new AARFAM have motion-sensitive lighting that covers each room overall and they are measuring the duration of the lighting. A time clock tracks the hours the lights are on and off. For example, in the textile gallery they are off 45 percent of the time even on a busy day. The museum is open 365 days a year, thirteen hours a day, with a visitation of 250,000 to 275,000 guests annually. So they are off nearly half the time at a high-traffic institution. That is a huge savings; think of how much more will be saved during slow times or could be saved in quieter museums. The advantage is that it allows CWF to maintain this conservative approach to collections care (reducing exposure to visible radiation), and to leave exhibitions of very light-sensitive materials on display longer, saving time, expense, and energy of installing new exhibits.

All of the lighting in the new AARFAM is controlled by a programmable system that includes controls for each lighting circuit, dimmers, and a time clock. Staff has agreed upon light levels for certain times of day and various tasks, such as cleaning or security walk-through, and when the gallery is open to visitors. The programming of various circuits and timing for their activation ensures that the lights are on only when needed. This saves electricity (and exposure of the collections) in the same way that a programmable thermostat does.

We cannot say enough about sensors. Efficiency is based on true need, not perceived need. Sensors help you achieve true service needs. At Phipps, sensors tell a computer system to open and close vents based on wind and temperature. This maximizes energy efficiency while giving the plants optimum growing conditions and helps the conservatory improve the efficiency of its irrigation methods. There is so much to be gained by monitoring systems and enabling them to manage systems automatically. It does not remove the need for trained staff and for constant monitoring, but it does dramatically improve efficiency.

McNeil points out that HVAC designers and engineers are constantly improving climate control systems to address very complex needs in lighting and in gallery temperature and air quality controls. He imagines a scenario with on-demand HVAC, similar to on-demand lighting. He is "arguing for a complete reassessment of those standards based on the minimal—yet safe—HVAC conservation requirements for exhibitions. We may find that conservation-safe climate control can be less stringent in certain environments and therefore less energy intensive."

He believes that in the near future museums will be forced to reevaluate lighting and climate control standards and embrace energy efficiency. Recent California Title 24 State building regulations, for instance, require rigorous energy efficiency standards. New museum construction projects will have to comply, and given the amount of lighting/HVAC required that will not be easy. The Crocker Art Museum in Sacramento has just been through the arduous process for their new addition, in the future it may impact existing museum buildings as well.

He points out that the California Lighting Technology Center at UC Davis has just developed the 100-watt kitchen: "a fully-equipped kitchen that uses a range of CFL and LED fixtures to generate all the kitchen's lighting needs using only 100 watts of electricity. It wasn't so long ago that a single lightbulb would require that much wattage. Now, if we can apply that type of thinking to an exhibition space, imagine what we could do." Green breeds that sort of innovation; public regulations may require it soon.

Energy Efficiency and Energy Generation

We all know that maintenance of specific and consistent environmental conditions is a fundamental precept of collections care for tigers and orchids, sea urchins and thirteenth-century panel paintings. We also have seen that maintaining these conditions takes a lot of increasingly costly energy. As green design has become mainstream, the marketplace has responded with very sophisticated and increasingly affordable energy efficient systems. High-performance, energy efficient systems (also those incorporating renewable energies such as wind and solar) are cost effective but also reliable—countering a frequently cited concern of curators. Biotechnical laboratories, hospitals, and other critical function facilities are building sustainably using these systems. If human lives hinge on the reliability of these systems, then tigers and orchids, sea urchins and thirteenth-century panel paintings can of course rely on them too.

In traditional office buildings the living things do go home at the end of the day, but at zoos, gardens, aquaria, and any museums with indoor spaces for living things, the living things stay. "Our animals never go home," says Joe Matyas, maintenance engineer for Cleveland Metroparks Zoo's Tropical Rainforest. That is because they are home: 600 of them live in sixty temperature zones on two acres in a two-story biosphere. And the objects and manuscripts stay. Most collecting museum facilities cannot depend on comprehensive night setbacks of systems as energy conservation measures. With that as a given, museums look elsewhere to reduce loads. In facilities without collections, however, you can institute setbacks. All museums can reduce consumption by paying attention to phantom loads. These are electronics (TVs), chargers (cell phones, etc.), and other devices (electric drills, etc.) that are drawing electricity in their standby mode. Connect these to a power strip that can be switched off when the devices are fully charged or not in use. Remember the mantra: reduce, reuse, and recycle. When it comes to energy (and water, but we will get to that later), reducing your load is the first step in any comprehensive energy management plan. As one facilities manager says, "I use the KISS method: Keep It Simple Stupid! Always remember, it's all about reducing energy consumption."

Energy Efficiency: Lighting

Reduce your electricity use through smart lighting systems in sync with available daylighting or daylight harvesting. Motion sensors work in offices, too. The Chesapeake Bay Foundation's Phillip Merrill Center has task lighting in addition to full-room overhead lighting controlled by daylight harvesting sensors. Watt-Stopper and others now specialize in dual-technology sensors that sense motion but also occupancy through changes in space temperature from body heat. You may choose to add light sensors on a few lights in a few places to test their feasibility at your museum, and to distribute the installation costs over a longer period, but they will pay for themselves and reduce harmful greenhouse gas emissions back at the electrical plant. Sensors on overhead lights measure daylight and dim lights accordingly. Now, with the widespread use of sensors we may all eventually forget how to turn off lights, but this automatic on-off is something we see on our car lights—why not everywhere else? In museums where computer systems automatically turn lights on or off, like at the Merrill Center, the Dewitt Wallace Gallery, or The Getty Center, there is an override on a timer that allows for special events or the late worker who wants to get in some extra time. Then the override timer turns off the lights.

Lighting in museums is a huge energy sink. Offices and support areas are one thing. But exhibition lighting tied to collections care has spawned an industry of specialized designers and increasingly sophisticated and energy efficient equipment. Automated lighting systems are just one component of addressing reduction of energy use. Lamps and fixtures are another and fortunately the marketplace has responded with a wide variety of products, and improvements are being made constantly. The Adirondack Museum is switching from traditional incandescent lightbulbs to CFLs (the corkscrew ones) and replacing the magnetic ballasts in fluorescent lights with more energy efficient electronic ballasts. There are two different concepts working here: efficiency of lighting (fluorescent vs. incandescent) and efficiency of ballasts (magnetic vs. electronic). Incandescent lights do not use ballasts, but fluorescents and CFLs do. Ballasts can be electronic, electromagnetic (hybrids), or magnetic, and their job is to start and manage the electricity flow into the lightbulbs. Electronic ballasts change the electric frequency, normally 60 hertz, to a more efficient level of about 25 kilohertz. This uses energy more efficiently. Now there are certain electronic ballasts for dimming fluorescent fixtures.

Fluorescent lights use gas that is "excited" with an electrical current. Exciting the gas takes less energy, initially and continually, than it does to heat the filament that produces light in an incandescent bulb. That means that the fluorescent light uses less electricity to create an equal amount of light (measured in lumens) and does so without adding heat to your building. Incandescent lights are really little heaters that also produce a bit of light. Depending upon whom you ask and what lights you use, the ratio is either 70 to 90 percent light, to 10 to 30 percent heat, with a CFL. With incandescent light the percentages are reversed: more heat compared to light for the energy spent.[12] The typical human produces 100 watts of heat, equivalent to a 100-watt incandescent lightbulb.[13] Now let's not hear you complaining about light color in exhibits. The lighting industry can provide comparable appearance light for almost every application, and they are researching the few they have not mastered.

As for CFLs, remember, they last eight, ten, or fifteen times longer than incandescents. Think how much less time you spend replacing those bulbs across their life span and across your entire institution. It is important to note: fluorescent lamps must, and CFLs should, be recycled because they contain mercury. In fact, keeping mercury out of buildings is an important green goal. Mercury is a toxic heavy metal and poses the greatest hazard to pregnant women, children, and infants and has been associated with the precipitous increase in autism over the last decade. The marketplace is responding to this concern and manufacturers are now offering more low-mercury-content CFLs with no sacrifice in longevity or performance. The first part of the message then is to pay attention to disposal of standard and compact fluorescent and sodium vapor lamps because of their high mercury content. Most vendors will take back your spent bulbs, but you may have to ask them to do it. There are mail-back programs for traditional fluorescent bulbs much like the recycling programs for toner cartridges. Many municipalities are adding recycling programs similar to those for batteries and pesticides. Go online to find out more about lamp recycling programs in your area. Part two of the lighting message is to continue to stay tuned

to the ever-expanding array of green lighting products that are being introduced on a regular basis.

Energy Efficiency: HVAC Systems

Energy efficiency through updating HVAC systems is a major capital project, what is often called the "high-hanging fruit" of greening any facility or
campus. When faced with maintenance and upgrades, maximize your return
on investment by tying your mechanical systems greening to institutional
capital, financial, and programmatic planning. Installing new, more efficient
air-conditioning or heating systems when the current one is only three years
old may not make any sense, but planning to do so when the current one
reaches twelve or eighteen years will.

Reduce energy consumption by rethinking availability and need. A critical component of energy reduction is the conceptual change from always
on to on-demand. For decades these terms have meant the same thing: if we
want lights in public places, leave them on all the time. If we want hot water
whenever we call for it, then the water heater has to be on all the time; not
so anymore. Consider tankless water heaters. They run on gas (natural or
propane) and need an electronic ignition, but they are not electric. They can
be up to 70 percent more efficient than traditional water heaters, running
only on demand, not 24-7. That means that the water gets heated when you
need it, not all the time. Think of the energy savings.

The twenty-five-year life expectancy of tankless water heaters bests traditional tanks, and they take up far less space.[14] For bathrooms, especially if
you have showers (for bikers or live-aboard boaters), these make excellent
sense. They are more expensive than traditional tanks, but energy savings
will cover the cost well before the tank is replaced, and the tank itself takes
up far less space in your building while reducing harmful emissions. You can
combine units or use high-capacity commercial units configured to meet
higher demands for bathroom areas and kitchens.

In your HVAC system, using variable frequency drives (VFDs, also
known as adjustable frequency drives and variable speed drives) saves
energy because the machines operate at the specific required load of the
system. They cycle less frequently if the demand is lower: fewer people, less
cooling. Variable drives do cost more than standard motor controls, but
energy savings cover that cost within the first year, and then continue to
save for the fifteen-plus years you can expect to operate them. Gilmore, at
CBMM, points out that "coupled with premium efficiency motors, VFDs
can dramatically reduce the electrical consumption associated with oper-

ating HVAC systems." Utilities often provide rebates exceeding the cost of installing VFDs and each new drive generation seems to be smaller and more efficient, too.

CBMM's main exhibit building has two fifteen-ton direct expansion chillers, each with a five-ton and ten-ton compressor. The combined units, thirty tons, were operating simultaneously. It was either all-on or all-off. Gilmore, who came recently to his job from a career managing university campuses, took a look at it, consulted with the manufacturer, and reprogrammed the system. With two ten-ton compressors and two five-ton compressors, a more efficient plan is to have them operate in sequence: five-ton first, then the five-ton shuts down and the ten-ton comes on; if needed the first five-ton can come back on, and then the next five-ton, and the machines can steadily increase capacity by five tons for each sequence. This was accomplished with a simple reconfiguration of four wires on the units' control panels. Instantaneously he reduced the electrical demand and energy associated with operating the facility. Load tailoring matches the variable demand placed on them. Traditional design has called for designing a system to handle the worst-case load scenario; tailoring a system to typical loads allows smaller units to run at their most efficient level, but with added small units to match peak needs when necessary.

CWF is a major historic site with hundreds of structures, old and new. The staff is conscious of the need to reduce energy costs and expects to realize its greatest gains in efficiency in the largest, newest buildings. The Dewitt Wallace Decorative Arts Museum, installed in association with a recreated public hospital building, is now twenty-two years old. The 2005 relocation of AARFAM to a portion of the Dewitt Wallace site provided an opportunity to consider new equipment; the necessary replacement of the failed fire suppression system at the Dewitt Wallace triggered a retrofit. The systems will, after a museum expansion project, employ VFDs that more appropriately match fan speed to condition demands. The refrigeration units serving the café will be precooled by the HVAC's chilled water return loop. Synergy among systems.

The Adirondack Museum campus at Blue Mountain Lake, New York, is thirty-three acres with twenty-two building and exhibit components. It is surrounded by 6 million acres of lakes and forests, towns, and villages known as the Adirondack Park. The website explains, "The history of the Adirondack Park—the place and its people—is at the heart of the museum's programs." The tagline, "History is our nature," is the perfect lead-in for green performance. Four of the major buildings share a heating plant by way of underground ducts. The efficiency of one quality system trumps the earlier separate systems. Air systems use variable speed fans and alternating air handlers to moderate electrical demand. Again, it is rarely all on, but is on as needed. Operations manager Mitchell Smith reports this reduces power consumption by half.

Green buildings often provide greater than average amounts of fresh air to occupied areas of the building to improve air quality. All that incoming air has to be warmed to room temperature. This can require a lot of energy, a particularly expensive proposition in cold climates. It seems like a waste to heat all this air and, after it is used briefly in the building, immediately dump it back outside. This is where heat recovery ventilators, also known as heat recovery units, are beneficial.

This mechanical equipment's job is to capture the heat from air expelled from the building and put it back into fresh incoming air. Enthalpy heat recovery units accomplish this by passing warm outgoing air through one or more giant heat exchange wheels. The Grand Rapids Art Museum (GRAM) uses a large heat recovery unit that contains three such wheels. At GRAM these disks are about twelve feet in diameter and resemble a giant wheel of cheese as they are composed of a very porous material that absorbs heat from the air passing through it. As this disk rotates slowly, one side removes heat from the expelled air while the other side deposits this heat into incoming unheated air. This is called preheating incoming air. It reduces demand on the heating system (and therefore saves energy) by warming cold outside air part of the way up to room temperature. This equipment is simple to operate and by capturing heat that would otherwise be dumped into the outdoor air, saves tremendous heat energy. The heat recovery ventilator at the Trustees of Reservations Doyle Conservation Center is designed to reduce the energy needed to heat incoming air by over 60 percent simply by capturing heat that would otherwise be lost. Heat recovery ventilators often pay for themselves in a few years through heating energy savings: Another good example of integrated design for energy efficiency.[15]

At the Brooklyn Children's Museum's new building sensors monitor carbon dioxide, occupancy, and daylight levels to automatically turn on and turn off systems for ventilation and lighting. The more visitors, the higher the CO_2 levels from their breathing; as the level rises it triggers a CO_2 sensor that turns on the fans for ventilation. The Getty Center uses the same system (VFDs on the fan motors) for regulating ventilation for carbon monoxide in its parking garage. With fewer visitors the fans run less. This ensures fresh air conditions without constant cycling and constant energy use. It is integrated design, or synergy among systems, at work again.

Energy Generation

When it comes to sustainable energy generation, there are old-fashioned options like wind and solar. There are also geothermal boreholes that provide heating and cooling by tapping the constant cool temperatures underground. There are fuel cells powered by hydrogen or natural gas. And, when you cannot make your own, you can buy green energy certificates from your utility like the Children's Museum of Pittsburgh, which generates or buys renewable power for 100 percent of its energy use. Innovation in renewable energy is moving at a rapid pace.

Some entrepreneurial spirits are thinking creatively: connecting their operations to energy production. The Dallas Zoo is doing just that. Chuck Siegel, the zoo's deputy director for animal management, says, "When you're in the zoo business, poo and pee is our bread and butter."[16] The plan to use animal waste for biogas generation is underway, thanks to a $10,000 Environmental Protection Agency grant for the waste-to-energy project. Projected costs are $750,000 to $1 million, but payback is significant. The project will save the zoo the cost of hauling six tons of waste a day and could help power several buildings at the zoo and provide irrigation to the landscaping. Creative synergy.

FUEL CELLS Phipps has a 5 kilowatt solid oxide fuel cell to run its new conservatory building (figure 3.3). A fuel cell makes energy. This one takes natural gas and creates electricity by exposing the hydrogen and added oxygen to electrodes and an electrolyte which separate the molecules to produce heat and water. The process is an electrochemical reaction that is two to three times more efficient in energy use (meaning more of the fuel is absorbed directly into energy not waste) than combustion is (burning fuel) and there are no emissions of nitrous oxide or sulfur oxide as with combustion. But wait, there's more! Any waste heat is captured to heat the water system and in the future they plan to pump the CO_2 into the greenhouses for the plants to convert. Fuel cells are expensive, and this was installed with significant financial support and as a prototype.[17]

PHOTOVOLTAIC (PV) PANELS Photovoltaics are becoming increasingly affordable, especially with state and local grants and utility subsidies. As the market responds they will become even more affordable. Until then, they can be a project that particular funders are interested in. In all cases they do produce energy that reduces energy outlays. The Los Angeles County Museum of Art (LACMA) is installing a grand entrance that has been spon-

FIGURE 3.3. Connect sustainability to your mission. One of the greenest gardens in the world, Phipps Conservatory and Botanical Gardens, has embraced sustainable building and operation practices. Their 2005 welcome center is LEED Silver and features energy- and water-use reduction measures, 100 percent wind power, and sustainable landscaping. Spanned by a green roof, their café serves local and organic foods, uses bio-based and recycled products, and vermicomposting for food waste. The 2006 Tropical Forest Conservatory project expanded the original 1893 landmark structure with revolutionary approaches to integrated design for energy efficiency and to operational practices that have raised the bar for conservatory design worldwide. The next phase in their expansion, new research, education, and administrative offices, is designed to exceed LEED Platinum. Photo by Paul G. Wiegman

sored by British Petroleum, the company with the green-and-yellow BP gas stations. When it is finished the roof over the pavilion will have solar panels to provide electricity for the museum.[18] The Art Institute of Chicago installed one of the largest PV arrays in the Midwest in 2002. The array produces electricity equivalent to that consumed by sixteen homes in one year.[19] The installation was supported by grants from the City of Chicago, the Illinois Department of Commerce and Community Affairs, and Commonwealth Edison (ComEd), the regional utility company.

In Massachusetts, a quasi-public agency (Massachusetts Technology Collaborative Renewable Energy Trust) offers grants for renewable energy feasibility studies and implementation. With help from Mass Tech, the Massachusetts Museum of Contemporary Art (MassMoCA) in North Adams installed a 50 kilowatt solar array, energy efficient equipment, and a related interactive exhibit on clean energy. The museum is in a huge, rambling New England mill and, as director Joseph C. Thompson says, "MassMoCA's energy costs—always staggering—have tripled (since 2003). ... And it's no exaggeration to say that the sustainability of this institution is linked to our success in finding radical cost savings in our utility bills." For grant recipients, it is easy to look at PVs as entirely a cost-saving measure. But it is important to remember the funder's viewpoint—the Mass Technology Collaborative is interested in promoting clean energy. Together they and the museum are satisfying both sets of needs.[20]

A generous individual donor approached the Adirondack Museum with the PV idea and contributed a significant portion of the funding. The New York State Energy Research and Development Authority's (NYSERDA) Photovoltaics on Buildings Program (PON 609) provided $118,000 of the $218,000 cost. A long roof over an existing exhibit wing provided a perfect south-facing surface, even at the correct angle, for installing the 1,800-square-foot photovoltaic system that is both roof and energy producer. Instead of applied panels, this is an integrated roofing and energy production system. Inside the exhibit hall, an existing utility room holds the computer for monitoring the system, and the nine Sunny Boy inverters, which look like normal electrical circuit breaker panels. They are mechanisms for changing the DC (direct current) that is generated by the solar array into AC (alternating current) for common use. Just outside the room an exhibit describes and interprets the panels, and provides a real-time, interpreted display of the energy levels produced by the photovoltaic system and used by the building. You can see the same display and learn more about the project on the museum's website. The system provides energy for use in the attached exhibit building and for sharing throughout the complex. They expect it to produce 21,000 kilowatt hours each year. The museum is adding a satellite location, ninety minutes away in downtown Lake Placid, New York, and plans to continue its sustainable practices with geothermal heating and a green roof.

The Science Museum of Virginia has parked the 2005 Solar Decathlon House built by Virginia Tech Students and faculty in its parking lot. The house was designed for the biennial competition in Washington, DC, that is hosted by the U.S. Department of Energy. At the Science Museum it is an exhibit on solar energy and sustainable construction. David Hagan, staff scientist, says one of the visitors' "aha" moments comes when they see the electric meter run backward—when it is generating excess electricity for the grid.

GEOTHERMAL The Brooklyn Children's Museum and Queens Botanical Gardens' (QBG) new visitor and administration building both use geothermal wells for their heating and cooling. Also called ground-source heat pumps, geothermal systems use the constant 55 degree temperature of water found deep within the earth. In summer this is cooler than the air, and in winter is warmer than the air that the museum would take in to heat or cool the building. By using this constant-temperature water to raise or lower the temperature of the air supplied to the buildings, it takes less energy to maintain a comfortable indoor temperature. Instead of working overtime to heat 25-degree winter air to room temperature, the geothermal wells and heat exchanger preheat the air to 55 degrees before the boiler takes over. This process is energy efficient in part because of water's density; water can absorb many times more heat than an equal volume of air.

Geothermal systems have the added advantage of operating almost silently. There are no noisy cooling towers to listen to or to try to hide from view, a plus given the Brooklyn Children's Museum's dense residential neighborhood. Instead the geothermal wells bring constant-temperature ground water to heat exchangers where its energy is used to heat or cool a separate loop of water that is circulated throughout the building. The groundwater is pumped back into the earth after the energy transfer is complete.

The Trustees of Reservations' Doyle Conservation Center (DCC) in central Massachusetts is also heated and cooled mechanically using a geothermal system. The geothermal system consists of two 1,500-foot-deep wells which supply ground water to a heat exchanger that in turn provides nineteen heat pumps throughout the building with tempered water as needed. The building also uses PV panels and other integrated design strategies to be 60 percent more energy efficient than a traditionally designed building of its same approximate 18,000-square-foot size. As in Queens and Brooklyn, the geothermal heat pump system at DCC is but one of several strategies aimed at load reduction as well as energy production.

On Cape Cod, the Provincetown Art Association and Museum has received LEED Silver for their renovation and expansion. Although the building was originally designed with a geothermal system, the project team ultimately decided to use high-efficiency furnaces after another ground-source system in Provincetown failed due to the groundwater's high mineral content. The lesson here is that buildings and system designs are location specific. Not every technology will work in every location.

Phipps uses earth tubes to manage heating, ventilation, and air conditioning in its Tropical Forest Conservatory. Six 300-foot, twenty-four-inch concrete tubes under the conservatory building work on a concept similar to the geothermal wells described above. Fifteen feet below ground the earth is 55 degrees year-round. Using the principle that hot air rises, hot air leaves the very top of the building, creating an upward draft that naturally draws in new air through the horizontal tubes. In summer the hot outside air is cooled as it passes through the tubes; in a Pittsburgh winter the Phipps only has to partially heat the air coming through the tubes. The new conservatory is 100 percent passively cooled. It does not have traditional air cooling or heating in the building at all.

Water Conservation and Management

Way back, folks had rain barrels to capture rainwater for use on gardens or for animals. Water was, and still is, a precious resource. Back to the three Rs—reduce, reuse, recycle. Start by using less, and then move on to harvesting water. This can be done with systems similar to rain barrels or you can capture runoff from your building. Garden and site managers know the value of water harvesting for landscape maintenance. As David Barnett, VP of operations and horticulture at Mount Auburn Cemetery (the nation's oldest park cemetery, dating to 1831) stated so plainly,

> Water is the single most important thing when dealing with our landscape. We try to be as efficient as possible and want to do more. We harvest rainwater from our greenhouse roofs and store it for watering our flower beds. Over the last few years we have gathered thousands of gallons of rainwater. We want to do more but for now are hindered by our storage capacity. As we move forward how we handle water will play a big role in everything we do.[21]

QBG uses a variety of strategies for water reduction, harvesting, and management. In fact the entire design of the new visitor's center and site revolves around water. Gray water (that used in sinks, dishwashers, and showers) is filtered through constructed wetlands and piped back into the visitor's center to be used for toilet flushing. Rainwater is harvested, cleansed, and used for a water feature and fountain on-site. Integration of building and site design-—beautiful.

Using less

Hopefully you can begin planting native plants with lower irrigation demands, but when you must irrigate, drip methods are far more efficient than traditional sprinkling. Drip irrigation provides a steady, gentle water supply at a rate the soil can absorb with very limited evaporation. That means the plant gets more of the water you intended for it. You will pump less, which conserves water and conserves energy to run the pumps. If you cannot install permanent drip irrigation, consider using drip hoses and moving them as needed. It is more intense for staff use, so you will have to evaluate its appropriateness, but it is an option.

For faucets it is inexpensive to add aerators: around $1 to $1.50 for each faucet, depending upon how many you buy. Aerators conserve water by mixing air with the water flow and reducing spray. Users can keep the water running for the usual time they need to wash their hands, but less water comes out of the faucet during that time, and none sprays outside the hand-washing radius and goes unused.

Installing low-flow toilets when you change out fixtures will reduce consumption. Dual-flush toilets give users the option to press the flush signal for low-water use for liquids, or for larger-volume water flush for waste solids. The Visitor Education Center at President Lincoln and Soldiers' Home National Monument and the Children's Museum of Pittsburgh both have dual-flush toilets.

Better yet, consider no water. Waterless urinals are a good way to go. Composting toilets truly work, and they are not unpleasant—really. They can be stand-alone models, or part of your main system. Frank Lloyd Wright's Falling Water in Mill Run, Pennsylvania, has a composting bathroom paid for by a donor (no name on the wall). State and national parks have been using them for remote toilets for years. The Chesapeake Bay Foundation's Merrill Center and The Trustees of Reservations' Doyle Conservation Center both use them as their only toilets in the buildings. They are part of the tour. The basement composting station is accessible. Guests are welcome to examine the finished compost. The advantages are avoided costs of installing and maintaining wastewater treatment system; avoided costs of managing black water; avoided costs of water purchase or sewage fees; reduced black water contribution to the environment; compost for use on your property or for sale; shall we go on?

Managing Storm Water

What is the big deal about storm water? The problem has three aspects: there is too much of it and it comes through fast and dirty. There is too much of it because we too often prevent its absorption by paving over the landscape with impermeable materials, leaving us with lots of water and no place to put it. The traditional response has been to let it flow into a storm drain and make its way untreated into the nearest watercourse. Well, if the storm's water, on its way from the cloud to the water source, falls through the air and onto an impermeable roof or parking lot, and then is gathered together to rush in volume into the pipes to the watercourse, it is going to collect pollutants from the atmosphere, pollutants off the roof or the tarmac, and carry it along at a rate and force that erodes the watercourse while dumping its dirty load. Storm water management is a combination of cleaning water through biological filters, slowing the flow by encouraging absorption and slowing the rate of flow to prevent erosion.

So green engineering encourages the reduction of impermeable surfaces by using green roofs and permeable pavement (the kind with gaps designed into the paving materials) to reduce runoff through absorption, and bioswales and rain gardens to hold larger volumes of water so the plants can filter it as it slowly seeps out. Then what reaches the watercourse arrives gently and cleaner. Museums accomplish this by creating green roofs (see next section) and parking and traffic areas with permeable pavers or porous pavement. The latter is a single-application material that allows water to seep through to recharge groundwater or be collected for filtering and managing through a storm drain system. These new kinds of pavement have larger aggregate—rock, pebbles, recycled glass, and so on—embedded in the binder that leaves gaps for water to infiltrate. Permeable pavers are bricks, cement forms, or plastic grids planted with grass that provide a mostly solid surface that has gaps for water seepage. There is a wide variety of these on the market and, for historic contexts, there are applications that resemble dirt surfaces. In the National Park Service's Minuteman National Historical Park in Massachusetts, the main road (the same road that witnessed the "shot heard around the world" and was the birthplace of our nation's freedom from British rule) looks much as it did in the eighteenth century yet is wheelchair accessible and stands up to all manner of weather conditions. It is also permeable.

Whatever surface you choose, it requires very careful engineering for climate, degree of use, materials and maintenance, and so on. Some formats require vacuuming—so be sure you understand the maintenance requirements. Rain that freezes on the road or walkway is a safety problem. Porous pavements often are drier with less chance of forming ice. This reduces your need for ice melt applications of chemical or sand, while improving safety. It will not be less expensive than traditional parking or other open surfaces, but if it eliminates the need for a full storm water management system, you will have related savings.[22]

The Adkins Arboretum will be installing porous pavement parking surfaces in its green renovation, and the plan calls for parking along the entrance drive rather than creating large square sections of wide-open parking. The distributed parking encourages visitors to take nearby paths through gardens and wetlands to reach the new visitors center. Take a moment to look at the ground in parking lots and you will notice new types of permeable paving and different kinds of pavers and paving systems that leave gaps for gravel or grass.

There is a dizzying amount of language to go with ditches designed to catch and clean water (rain garden, bioswale, etc.). The main issues are holding water, cleaning water, and how much water the system can handle. Your engineers will fill in the blanks, but you need to know that these man-made vegetated wetlands are designed to hold water for a variety of benefits—absorption, filtration, or slowed runoff. The most attractive ones are planted with vegetation that provides color, texture, and natural filtration. You do not have to settle for open ditches or ponds. Create an attractive space that encourages programming or provides beauty and opportunities for relaxation and pleasure.

The Trustees of Reservations' Doyle Conservation Center sits amid 200-plus acres of protected landscape. Storm water mitigation on-site was achieved through a series of wet meadows which clean runoff and create a diverse meadow habitat before the overflow reaches a wetland north of the project site. The planting design reestablished several native plant communities. Three years postoccupancy, building users reported that the constructed wetlands are also habitat for herons, bobolinks, and other local species.

Keeping It Cleaner

Sustainability in water use means using less, reusing more, and keeping it all cleaner. Bioswales, rain gardens, and green roofs and walls can make the gray water and storm water cleaner, but what about black water—the stuff from the toilets? There are septic systems and living machines. Septic systems we already know about: they reduce the sewage and water the public systems have to manage by treating much of it on-site and holding the solid waste for collection and treatment. Since Blue Mountain Lake, New York, does not provide a sewer system, the Adirondack Museum has its own septic system to treat waste. With Blue Mountain Lake below the museum as the community's water source, treating sewage and returning water to the lake as clean or cleaner than when it came out is obviously important for the museum, its guests, and its home community. You can argue that it is mandated, but it is an environmentally benign situation. How could we upgrade this?

Consider a Living Machine. Phipps is installing a water treatment system during the next phase of upgrades. A Living Machine processes the black water on-site and returns it for any use. It is a sequence of tanks with microorganisms, plants, and animals that break down the materials and filter the water to drinkable quality. Since the mental leap is a bit much for us all, this sort of water is most often reused for toilets, not drinking, but it is completely cleaned and contained on-site. Corkscrew Swamp Sanctuary, a part of the National Audubon Society's sanctuary system, is the largest remaining stand of virgin bald cypress trees in the world. The sanctuary built a Living Machine in 1994. It can handle up to 10,000 gallons of wastewater daily. It is an exhibit that is fully accessible to the public, somewhat humbly built in a screened enclosure near all the visitor amenities.[23]

Chlorine kills animals with semipermeable membranes like fish and frogs. You can dechlorinate with chemicals, or you can do it naturally. On-site water reservoirs allow institutions dependent upon city water to hold water days in advance to dechlorinate it by naturally allowing the water to off-gas chlorine through the surface or with the help of an airstone (bubbler). Steve Smith at ECHO points out the value of water reservoirs for dechlorination and energy efficient management of multiple water temperatures. But there is a catch. Your municipal water may contain chloramine, a form of chlorine created specifically to avoid loss of chlorine in pipes on the way to the consumer. This will not off-gas, so you will have to treat it.

One more note about keeping the water clean. Soap is not good for things that live in water. Even biodegradable soap is not good. It breaks down, but is still toxic to fish. We should use biodegradable soap rather than detergent until we find a better remedy, but still be sure the soap runs through treatment (natural or mechanical) before it reaches a water source. So please wash vehicles and the outside tables on a grass or gravel surface to trap the soap, or make sure it all runs through a water treatment system.

Green Roofs and Walls

Green Roofs

Some sustainable systems are just about energy efficiency. Green roofs may improve energy efficiency inside the building depending upon your climate, but their greatest value is storm water management and replacement of asphalt with green. By providing a vegetated cover that does not absorb heat, your systems may not have to work so hard to cool the building, but the real heat issue is the reduction in the heat island effect of a dark-colored, heat-absorbing roof. If you are not creating a hovering air mass 70 to 85 degrees warmer than the surrounding air, you are helping the air temperature sur-rounding your site. Imagine how that improves conditions in a very urban situation. The living roof also absorbs rainfall, slowing the storm water release by evapotranspiration into air over time, and by filtering and slowly releasing cleaner water through gutters and downspouts to your gray water system or to rain gardens or a nearby water system.

New structures and substantial historic structures have roof systems that often can hold the green roof system with little or no modification, but if your roof has been built within the last fifty years, you may have to do some retrofitting. It is not that the medium is so heavy, but that the construction methods are often less substantial in modern buildings than in historic ones. Your contractor should point out that you still have to build a roof, and you will have to be able to water the plants. A green roof requires:

❖ The primary roof structure
❖ The waterproof and root-resistant membrane
❖ An inorganic layer (there are many types from loose materials to eggcarton–style sheets) that allows air access to roots and some water retention space
❖ Engineered planting medium (growing matter that is lighter than traditional soil)
❖ The plants
❖ Irrigation arrangements—formal or informal, shall we say

The payback is in longevity and reduced environmental impact. What you build will last three to five times longer than traditional roofing. A green roof does not suffer UV-related damage or the more intense expansion and contraction from heat extremes, so roofing materials and membranes last far longer. With advances in technology, vendors have created lightweight mate-rials and formats that make the green roof and planting mediums far lighter than you would imagine, so do not assume a green roof is not for you.[24]

The variety of plant options is astounding. If you build an "extensive" roof, you can plant grasses and sedums that require less care and maintain a low profile. Often these are nonaccessible roofs. An "intensive" roof is more parklike and able to support shrubs and trees. This means you can use it for education programs and demonstration gardens, cultivation events, and facilities rental; just remember it requires the maintenance levels of a park. Sometimes these roofs qualify for park-designated funds for construction and maintenance.

Green roofs are almost common now. The Mashantucket Pequot Museum and Research Center in Connecticut installed one in 1998. The Getty Center, the Rock and Roll Hall of Fame, the California Academy of Sciences, the Children's Museum of Boston, the Visitor and Administration Center at the Queens Botanical Garden, and the Clinton Presidential Library all have them. But you do not have to be big: the Havre de Grace Maritime Museum is creating an exhibit space green roof. Brenda Dorr Guldenzopf, executive director, was looking to make green changes as a way to lead by example and use green to teach, but pulling together all the pieces was a challenge. The museum is small and sits on leased land in a city setting at the edge of the Chesapeake Bay. The goal was a green roof on its new pavilion—a combination roof and living exhibit. The museum wants to be "an example of sustainable design" and Guldenzopf says that it is important "especially since we are situated next to the Bay and want to exemplify green practices." With its location next to the city's Promenade and Concord Point Lighthouse, which are the most popular destinations in the city and county, it will have terrific visibility. Guldenzopf began attending sessions about green design in 2002 or so, and found a local resource that pushed the project from idea to implementation: in her county a vendor grows plants for green roof planting. That meant not only was the vendor nearby for maintenance support, but that the museum could buy locally—an important green tenet.

The green roof at the Peggy Notebaert Nature Museum in Chicago has lots of bells and whistles—enough to win a 2003 Chicago Green Roof Award. The museum has chosen to be "the premier museum focused on the Midwestern environment" and to be "an exemplar as well as an advocate." This roof is not built to hold the public, but it is visible to the public and accessible for researchers and maintenance. Their drip irrigation system has a solar-driven pump. There are eighty species of plants, and the terrain ranges from a bit of wetland to ten inches tall. John Krueger, a horticulturist and educator on green roofs and other sustainable practices, says it can reduce heat loss due to wind up to 50 percent—an important energy efficiency in their prairie-like location. Your results may vary depending upon climate, orientation, and many other factors. Krueger says in general an extensive green roof can add 25 percent insulation to your building, and the

Notebaert's reduced needs for natural gas heating and cooling are a testament to that.

Green or Living Walls

The Notebaert museum also has a living cliff, as they call it. It is an exterior exhibit and a building element. Both require maintenance and the staff says they have struggled recently with finding the correct irrigation to keep all the plants alive, but they are committed to tweaking the system until they solve the problem. Living cliffs or walls are not very common in museums or many other American buildings yet, but already there is great variety. Some simply are vertical plantings; others are air and water systems. You might want to consider any version in your entrance areas (inside or out) and larger reception areas. They make a dramatic statement and can serve multiple purposes simultaneously.

A living wall is one that is planted; some call it vegetated. It can be indoors or out, and it can be attached to the air system or the water system or neither. It depends upon what you want to achieve. If it is attached to the water system, then as gray water travels down through the plant attachment material, the plant roots clean the water. If it is attached to the air system, then as the air filters through the plant attachment material, the plant roots clean the air. If the living wall is on the exterior (usually not attached to systems for cleaning air or water) it can be less expensive to build than a brick face. The living matter provides great insulation year-round, reduces solar heat gain because there is no thermal mass (wall material to absorb heat), and in the growing season the photorespiration action cools the surface.

Landscape and Maintenance Practices

The first principle of sustainable landscaping is to use native plants. They require less water, fewer chemicals, and less care to thrive. This saves you money on labor and systems and chemicals. The Children's Museum of Pittsburgh and the Visitor's Education Center at President Lincoln and Soldiers' Home National Monument have installed no-irrigation landscaping. Native plants can be a part of your garden plan for collecting and cleaning storm water, and are attractive and educational landscape features that require less maintenance than do ornamentals. Native plants also contribute to biodiversity by promoting regional plants that ornamentals may crowd out. Take the time to learn what are the native plants for your area and how best to use them in attractive and functional plantings on-site.

The Notebaert Museum restored four acres of prairie. Krueger cautions that the best method for prairie planting is to work with an experienced installer, to replace or rebuild soil strata appropriately, and plant using plugs instead of seed. (The same goes for replacing subaquatic vegetation for living shorelines.) Maintenance for the prairie includes prescribed burns. Krueger says it evolved in nature as the best way to keep down weeds: "native plants thrive because they're adapted in a way weeds are not." If you are not ready to install a prairie and it is not native to your area anyway, at least consider limiting lawns unless they create a historic sense of place or you use a reinforced one for overflow parking. Lawns require intense chemical use and mowing (which usually requires burning fossil fuels).

Many landscape managers have eliminated chemical fertilizers and pesticides by using integrated pest management practices. Many have also found a cost savings in materials and labor by allowing fallen leaves to remain in place rather than take up the leaves and then put them in composting bins and use it later for mulch. Now, changes in the design of mower blades enable staff to pulverize that material in place and allow the natural organic matter and nutrients to return to the soil. It is obviously an old system.

Managing Vegetation

The Minuteman National Historical Park (MA) employed an old-new idea for clearing open space: sheep. On overgrown and wooded lands in Concord, Lincoln, and Lexington, a combination of sheep munching and tree clearing helped the land resume its 1770s open-field appearance. The added benefits were the increased rural feeling in the park and the dramatic reduction in visitors' poison ivy exposure.

The Getty Center for the last three years, even before the LEED-EB process, has hired 300 goats for weeks of work—eating brush. Think fire. The goats take over the acres of chaparral-covered hillsides, mowing down the brush in rugged areas where the terrain is a serious risk to grounds crews. That means the staff can avoid the rough hillsides, rattlesnakes, and wasp nests. Reducing the fire fuel on the hillsides is a critical safety responsibility that protects the center, its collection, and its neighbors. Without the weed whackers, the neighborhood is happier and there are no internal combustion engines amid the fire-dry brush. The practice is energy efficient, safe, and has marvelous human value. The neighbors love the goats and visit with them over the fence. The goats are there long enough to deliver their kids during spring. The center staff eats lunch outside near the goats and develops serious attachments. They even named one kid J. Paul. The herds at Minuteman National Park and The Getty Center require shepherds and guard dogs to oversee them and enough acreage to make a herd an appropriate management tool, but it has excellent payoff in managing the landscape and appealing to visitors and neighbors.

Green Open Space

CWF has placed conservation easements on 230 wooded acres it owns near the entrance to the city of Williamsburg. Those acres are now permanent green buffers between the real world and the museum. Now, as it sells that land, the foundation is realizing a much smaller return on the property. It was able to compensate by taking the tax credits allowed for up to 50 percent of the diminution in the land's value, and selling them to tax-paying entities. The buyer may not pay the full value of the credit, but the payment does provide a financial balm alongside the environmental gain for the museum and its community. This is not an option in every state, however, and in Virginia the law was recently changed to reduce the tax credit to 40 percent of the diminution in value. The foundation will divest itself of other property, with significant easements, in order to protect viewsheds and the environment, says Victoria Gussman, director of property planning and management.

The Seattle Art Museum (SAM) has changed the landscape of its city by turning a former brownfield into a free public sculpture park. The former site of the Union Oil Company of California (UNOCAL) facility sits on the Seattle shoreline of Elliott Bay. The company loaded and unloaded petroleum products here for sixty-five years. In 1999 SAM, with the Trust for Public Land, purchased the site. Then in 2000, with financial help from the city of Seattle and King County, SAM and the Museum Development Authority purchased an abutting lot and prevented the construction of a private building that would have limited public access to the park and the water, and interfered with the panoramic view of Puget Sound and the Olympic Mountains. There were few parks and no large community gathering spaces downtown before the park was developed. That need inspired the multi-entrance design so that, in SAM's words and deeds, "the city literally flows through the park and the park flows through the city." Now Olympic Park's boardwalk and paths provide public access to the waterfront, an extension of a public bicycle trail, and a replanted shoreline to support salmon restoration. With a generous operations endowment from Jon and Mary Shirley, the park is free to the community.

In Norman, Oklahoma, the Sam Noble Oklahoma Museum of Natural History at the University of Oklahoma recently added more than twenty acres of open space to the state's Natural Areas Registry to conserve a prairie hay meadow. In addition to being one of the few meadows remaining in central Oklahoma, the site also hosts a large population of Oklahoma beardtongue, a beautiful and threatened flowering plant found only in central Oklahoma.

Fruitlands Museum in Harvard, Massachusetts, owns and manages over 200 acres of open space with stunning views over the Nashoba Valley. Home to Native American and Shaker communities, and an important site of the Transcendentalist movement, there is a special sense of place that has made the museum a draw since its founding in 1914. As development has started to creep into the valley, the museum has moved beyond its traditional purview of caring for its collections of Native American and Shaker materials and American nineteenth-century paintings to more proactively care for and program its landscape (a meadowland restoration project was just completed) and to speak on behalf of the viewshed. Light pollution and megastructures threaten the view and the museum has served as a rallying force for other like-minded conservation and cultural groups in the area.

Green Historic Preservation

Betty Arenth, senior vice president of the Senator John Heinz History Center, says, "We're a history organization. Think about it: It's preservation of the environment for the future."

Sustainable practices are old concepts. History museums have direct alignments with them: catching water in rain barrels and cisterns, using reading and work lamps instead of overhead lights (task lighting, not room lighting), capitalizing on the natural terrain and solar orientation for siting buildings, getting by with less, reusing what we could, and recycling everything else. The language may be new, and the concept refashioned, but it is not new to use available resources to suit our needs with little or no cost to the environment or our bottom line.

There is a reason farmhouses sit out in the middle of the fields surrounded by tall shade trees. Windows, before air-conditioning, had movable sashes, large openings, and were positioned to provide cross-ventilation. Think of the old mills: sited on a waterway for power. Seems basic, yes? Well, the old technology has its place in modern green practice. The Gibson Mill in Yorkshire, England, is a nineteenth-century cotton mill owned by the National Trust. It generates its own power with no link to the national grid. It supplies its own water and manages its own waste.[25] The trust revived the mill's original water system to provide energy for the building. Two turbines, an original large turbine and a smaller one hooked to the photovoltaic roof panels (for spring and summer lower water levels) provide the power and charge an 80 kilowatt storage battery for four days of backup. And it can all be interpreted to the public. So feel free to label, or interpret, a modern version of a historically energy efficient or sustainable practice to help your guests make the same connection between the wind turbine and the old windmill water pump, the gray water you use on the landscape and the dishpan water that was once dumped on the kitchen garden, and between your radiant heating and the technology of Roman baths.

The Children's Museum of Pittsburgh reuses two historic structures and built a green connector. They capitalized on recycled and reused materials, with 50 to 75 percent of the materials coming from local salvage companies or a nonprofit that resells construction components like stained glass windows, floorboards and wall panels, light fixtures, cabinetry, and carpet. When CWF wanted to create a new setting, in a more appropriate location, for the Abby Aldrich Rockefeller Folk Art Museum, they recycled the existing building into a spa and built the new building on an existing footprint at the Public Hospital complex immediately adjacent to the Dewitt Wallace Decorative Arts Museum.

On an idea from a volunteer, the Fresnel lens in the 1879 Hooper Strait Lighthouse standing on Navy Point at the Chesapeake Bay Maritime Museum now runs on a sixteen-watt compact fluorescent bulb: preservation and conservation in action. Green does not cancel out historic preservation. It can exist in complete harmony. Existing buildings are greener than new construction. The embodied energy in a building (all the energy that went into finding the materials, bringing them to the site, and building the building) is wasted when you tear it down and fill a dump with it. Then you will just spend more energy to find new materials, bring them to the site, and build a new building. If you consider both processes in the equation, the new building costs all of the old building plus the new building. So, recycle your buildings.

Merging green design with best practices in historic preservation and adaptive reuse is a growth area. Preservationists have been quick to point out that preservation and reuse of existing buildings is in itself a green activity. However, as green designers have become more savvy and the materials and systems marketplace has offered more choices, the merging activity is getting easier. To date the oldest building in the country to receive a LEED Gold rating is an 1871 former school adapted for municipal offices by the city of Cambridge, Massachusetts. Boston's Trinity Church, H. H. Richardson's architectural masterpiece and home to stunning John LaFarge decorative painting and stained glass, uses geothermal wells for heating and cooling. The Trustees of Reservations' Old Manse (historic home of Ralph Waldo Emerson) in Concord, Massachusetts, has composting toilets and the organization is exploring a variety of energy reduction strategies at many other of its historic properties.

As more case studies come out, and more owners and architects learn about the possibilities, we will surely see a rapid increase in green historic preservation. The Association for Preservation Technology (APT) has formed a Technical Committee on Sustainable Preservation. *The APT Bulletin: The Journal of Preservation Technology* is a good disseminator for best practices and recent preservation conferences have seen an uptick in the number of sessions on the topic. Certainly the National Trust for Historic Preservation and the National Park Service are also learning and sharing important information with the field. Changes to the USGBC's LEED program will allow for more flexible application of the credits to accommodate the specialized needs of historic preservation. Increased adoption will in turn spur the marketplace, encouraging owners around the cost effectiveness of green historic preservation and adaptive reuse.

Green Transportation

Transportation is a huge part of the environmental sustainability challenge: how your staff and visitors get to your site, and how you move people around your site and related sites. Alternate transportation includes bicycle racks for employees (with showers available, too); incentivized car and van pools, and public transportation passes for staff; bicycles, electric golf carts, or other small vehicles for getting around the complex; electric trams for moving visitors; and alternative fuel bus systems.

The Getty Center earned LEED-EB credits because of access to public transportation, bike racks and shower/changing rooms, and by creating an alternate transportation program. The Getty heavily subsidizes a van pool program as an employee benefit that decreases the parking needed. That decrease in cars equals a decrease in the energy consumed since air handlers cycle less frequently to remove carbon monoxide in the parking garage than they would for higher parking capacity. As for alternative fuels, The Getty Center's contracted visitor shuttle service for remote lots has considered biodiesel, but there will not be a filling station close enough until the summer of 2008.

Explore every opportunity. CWF has a fleet of buses. They circle the historic area in Williamsburg continuously and they currently travel on to Yorktown and Jamestown. They are diesel—or they were. The staff, visitors, and residents had long complained that the buses were noisy, dirty, and smelly. A change to cleaner buses "was the right thing to do," says Kurt Reisweber, fleet manager. The local gas company, Virginia Natural Gas, was interested in growing its business, so it provided an incentive, a low-cost loan, for CWF to build a fueling station. CWF had a three-to-five-year buy-back time frame. The fueling station cost about $300,000 for the three compressors plus the costs of concrete pad, piping, and fill posts (counterparts of traditional gas pumps), not to mention running the gas service. That is a lot of investment. To make it worthwhile requires a critical mass of buses: CWF now runs twenty natural gas buses, off its peak of twenty-seven during 2007. Congressional earmarks, a state grant, and National Park Service funding in support of the Jamestown 400th anniversary celebrations in 2007 provided for purchase of sixteen buses by adjacent James City County that CWF leases and runs among the three towns. It is still not an inexpensive proposition for CWF, but it was an important commitment to the community. CWF wanted to clean up its practice and many entities worked to make it possible.

It is now considering low-speed electric trucks for maintenance use in the historic area. The truck beds are small and so are unequal to many tasks, but the vehicles are more useful than electric golf carts, which in most cases are not allowed on the public streets adjacent to the historic area. In researching these trucks Reisweber will speak with other users to identify potential pitfalls. When CWF considered electric buses they discovered that with the length of their route, the buses would have to be pulled offline to recharge during the day. That just does not fit their needs in such a high-demand area. The lesser demands of some historic area projects suit the electric trucks, though, which can recharge in eight hours (overnight) through a regular outlet. Of course the electricity is expensive, and dirty if created from coal and not mitigated by carbon offsets, but that will all be part of the decision matrix. As the green industry addresses these problems, perhaps the pickups will come to work on solar power or power derived from renewable sources.

Green Education: Connecting the Dots

Integrating interpretation or an educational program into every green action is effective mission enhancement (even a worm composting bin can be an exhibit), leads to engaging the public in activities that preserve the environment, and connects you to audiences who are growing up green. Interpretation and programming is the easiest place to begin green activities.

CBMM is at the beginning of its transition to a green campus, and it has begun with programming. The museum held its first Bay Day (think Earth Day) in early 2007. The staff expected about twenty-five environmental organizations to set up booths for the public information day; eighty showed up. They ranged from grassroots to international, and all provided facts and inspiration to encourage individuals to help save the Bay with at-home activities and volunteer opportunities. As always the shared experience creates opportunities for next-step activities. The museum partners with Creek Watchers, volunteers who monitor development, residential practices, and any other conditions on the thousands of miles of creek tributaries to the Chesapeake Bay, and now lead water-based museum tours for visitors and members ready to take to kayaks for a new view. CBMM teamed up with the Adkins Arboretum, forty-five minutes away, for a workshop on building rain gardens. The museum now offers programs for waterfront homeowners on creating living shorelines and provides public lectures via kayak. The museum picked up a photographic exhibit on marshes and expanded it with lectures, photography classes, and water tours. The list is longer, but you get the jist.

To reconnect to the water, the museum is adding a living shoreline when it replaces traditional shoreline construction with angled stone barrier construction surrounded by restored subaquatic vegetation, backed by graded shoreline infill that is planted with native grasses. The living shoreline restores the appearance of a natural shoreline while creating a sturdy barrier to mitigate wave action from tides and boaters, and leaving access for aquatic creatures between water and land. When the museum begins planting and propagating oysters, popularly known as oyster gardening, the shoreline will be an interpretive site above and below water. The living shoreline will link the indoor exhibits on waterfowling, wildlife, and Chesapeake Bay life and work with natural landscapes for interpretation. Interpretation starts with construction and modelling—how to build responsibly.

The Chesapeake Bay area has thousands of miles of shoreline along bayside, creeks, and rivers. With that much shoreline, thousands of people live at the water's edge and share responsibility for its management. CBMM held a free workshop on greening nonprofit campuses where a speaker discussed living shorelines and the plans for installing them at the museum. One participant recognized that when the shoreline on his property is rebuilt by the county in the coming months, its solid-wall structure will block access to the shore. In this case this means that breeding terrapins cannot reach their nesting grounds. As a species of concern in Maryland, that is considered endangered in nearby states, this is a serious issue. Now that the landowner knows there are options, he will document the situation and take it to the state. Your audience is all around you. Walking the talk will make a huge difference.

Anything is a target for programmatic outreach. The Bronx Zoo uses signage throughout its campus to draw connections between visitors' lives and behaviors, and the zoo's conservation mission; for example, there are signs near the aviary about ways to help birds in urban and suburban areas. Seizing the opportunity to address a captive audience, other signage underscores the conservation idea in the zoo's eco-restroom, located just inside the zoo's Bronx River Parkway entrance, where 60 percent of the zoo's 2 million annual visitors enter and exit (Figure 3.4). It opened on Earth Day 2007 and was produced with a tight budget using simple design and materials. The project was selected as 2007 Environmental Project of the Year by GreenBuildings NYC. Featuring images and text from the children's book *The Truth about Poop* by Susan Goodman and illustrated by Elwood Smith, the clever signage exhorts guests to deposit their "liquid assets" and conveys a clear conservation message in practical (and humorous) terms. The signage explains that the composting toilets use only three ounces of water and a cascade of biocompatible foam, while a conventional toilet uses nearly two gallons of water per flush. A gray water harvesting system takes excess water from the sinks and filters it through the garden outside where more labels offer visitors tips on water conservation and outline why it is important. Conservation practice can be educational practice.

There is no need to limit programming to on-site or to traditional formats. The Peggy Notebaert Nature Museum in Chicago has a great series of web pages on its green activities, including a kids' activity on green roofs. Green is great for online or instructor-led question-and-answer activities or decision-making trees. Since any environmental decision affects many aspects of daily life, you could create a program each month on what happens to (storm water, poop, garbage) or where (energy, water, wood, plastic, etc.) comes from. The museum has offered a free workshop on green parenting, an online publication on green gifts for the holidays, and a tree-recycling service. What about creating a variant on traditional admissions fees by accepting CFL lightbulbs on weekends until you have all the lightbulbs you need? Arrange with a merchant to promote the program in-store to sell lightbulbs and increase your visibility. For visitors who come without a lightbulb, sell bulbs on-site and encourage guests to buy them for their homes. You can take it a step further by providing twice-annual CFL recycling.

Where Does It End? It Doesn't!

If you are involved in a green construction project or a green renovation project, it is tempting to see the project as an event—you design it, build it, and open it—but sustainability is not permanent. Maintaining energy efficiency and environmental sustainability requires monitoring to demonstrate performance and identify areas for repair or improvement, updating to take

FIGURE 3.4. Practice what you preach. The Bronx Zoo helps visitors make the green connection in their eco-restrooms, located at one of the zoo's busiest entrances. The building features green design strategies (daylighting, small footprint, eco-friendly building materials as well as water efficient fixtures: the composting toilets use 99 percent less water than conventional ones) and the landscape serves as a demonstration of gray water recycling. Signage uses humor to share facts about poop and explains the importance of water conservation and connects it to everyday actions that visitors can institute. Interestingly, exhibit evaluators and developers at the zoo report the lessons learned at the eco-restroom have had a transformative effect on the institution. They now see the educational potential of every space at the zoo, reaching beyond the confines of traditional exhibition spaces, with mission-connected messages about conservation to encourage visitors to change their own practices and be mission messengers as well. Photo by Julie Larson Maher © WCS

advantage of advances in technology, and adaptation to respond to new uses of the property and new demands from legislation, staff, and visitors. Commissioning—testing the system to be sure it is working as designed and as needed—is a big part of that. "God forbid museums don't do the commissioning," says Sheridan. It is the old penny-wise and pound-foolish idea. One museum gave a presentation on their new green development at AAM, complete with descriptions of the water conservation and energy efficiency measures. During the question and answer session, a question was asked about whether or not the project was seeking LEED certification. The response was no because LEED requires commissioning and the budget was tight, so it was cut. This for some folks clearly illustrated a missed opportunity. Those who know the value of commissioning also know that all the wonderful outcomes described in the presentation would likely not come to pass unless commissioning, indeed ongoing monitoring and evaluation, was valued and understood to be critical. Remember the engineer who said going green was like adopting a healthy lifestyle to lose weight, not a diet where you consider your task done and then promptly gain the weight back.

We cannot overstate the importance of monitoring systems. The museum field has learned well the lesson of measuring performance to evaluate success and plan future action. Measuring performance in green behavior is just as critical and perhaps simple once the process is in place. Efficiency is not a permanent condition. Joe Matyas, maintenance engineer at the Cleveland Metroparks Zoo, writes, "we must continue to make sure we do not become complacent about buildings that were designed to be energy efficient, but through the years have become less so. We must always keep one eye on advances in technology, and the other on the building systems."[26]

The Adirondack Museum's photovoltaic cells are monitored by a New England vendor. The monthly reports help the museum and the company manage the system. When report data showed anomalies in output, they could be attributed to a failed inverter and to a snow cover problem. With the inverter repaired, one problem was solved. Snow cover is usually eliminated naturally and "fairly quickly" by the solar array itself;[27] however, in years of unusual snow coverage it can interrupt solar power generation.

Steve Smith, director of animal care and facilities at ECHO, oversees the software programs that monitor ECHO's systems. There are three parts of the sophisticated around-the-clock operation system. The first monitors heating, air-conditioning, and life support for the fish. The second is an alert program that sends warning alerts to Steve's pager. The third is a package that monitors the lighting systems. The programs offer real-time and seasonal comparisons for assessing systems performance, keep historical data for management records, and identify energy savings. After initial training on the software Steve acquired most of his understanding simply by using the system. He is particularly pleased with the lighting system software and the energy it saves. Adjustments to systems are now business as usual four years into the building's history. For the first two years contractors did regular reviews and maintenance of the systems. Now Steve and his small maintenance staff can address nearly all the issues with occasional support from the contractors. The computerized systems not only save energy but save a great deal of personnel and utility costs.

Matyas recommends diligence in simple efforts like maintaining the insulating qualities of airlocks on entrance doors and caulking on windows; continued training of maintenance staff; and being ready for new state-of-the-art systems when the time comes. Monthly reviews and quarterly reports provide data trends to help you recognize areas that need retuning or updating. The action plans that accompany your long-range plan should include energy efficiency goals as part of overall sustainability goals.

There is always another exhibit to install, a program to try, a product for the gift shop, a utility bill to review, a system to replace. You will quickly learn to view each as an opportunity to increase your institution's environmental sustainability. If you monitor what you do, you will have a great score card for celebrating your performance.

Policy

Each of the institutions in this book is in a different stage of implementing sustainable practices. Few have policies on environmental sustainability, but most realize policy is critical for success. Colleges and universities, and many corporations, are far ahead of museums in this effort. We believe that policies on environmental sustainability will soon become a professional expectation for all types of organizations, not just museums.

Policy institutionalizes behavior by providing vision and frameworks, defining process, identifying goals and evaluation methods, and delegating authority. You may create a policy that stands alone or one that is woven into existing policies. What matters is that it provides a responsive framework for decision making. CBMM is learning about sustainable behavior and policy and is drafting policy. CWF has an expectation of sustainable behavior across the organization; so far it has been applied on a case-by-case basis, but eventually it will work its way into policy. MBAq has had a policy on environmentally sensitive business practices for nearly a decade. It is very sophisticated and far-reaching and we have reproduced it here in its entirety as an important resource. Policies at OMSI and Madison Children's Museum are good examples to start with, too.

To develop your own, spend some time on the web reading policies for colleges and universities, and for museums. Consider the scope and format for each; review the associated action plans; and consider the kinds of ripple effects sustainability decisions have on all aspects of your organization from mission and finances to products and results. Develop the policy in draft form and plan to revisit it in six months to finalize and then yearly to update. Like your other policies, one on environmental sustainability will be unique to your institution, but will have components in common with other museums.

Monterey Bay Aquarium Policy Statement: Environmentally Sensitive Business Practices

5/19/99

Purpose

The purpose of this document is to ensure that the aquarium's daily business operations reflect and advance its conservation mission. This policy statement is intended to provide a framework for the Board and the staff to guide continuous improvement in the area of environmentally sensitive business practices.

Statement of Principles

We recognize that, as an institution with large numbers of visitors, employees and volunteer staff, our environmental footprint is significant. We seek to adhere to the highest principles of environmental responsibility in all our operations, adopt administrative procedures and fiscal policies that put those principles into practice and, through our practices, set an example for colleagues seeking to integrate conservation practices into their own operations.

Institutional Commitment and Oversight

The aquarium's Conservation Committee, comprised of staff from throughout the organization, is charged with making recommendations to senior management that improve the environmental sensitivity of our business practices; encouraging and rewarding staff involvement in environmentally sensitive business practices; and communicating these practices to aquarium staff. One member of the senior management Leadership Council, the Director of Conservation Research, sits on the Conservation Committee. The committee meets monthly to set goals, monitor progress and oversee aquarium conservation programs.

IV. Operational Areas of Focus

A. Reduce, Reuse and Recycle
Conservation starts by reducing consumption of new materials; extending the life of materials through reuse; recycling of materials with no further useful life; and purchasing of items

made from recycled materials to foster demand for recycled products. Specific operational policies include:

1. Source reduction & reuse: All vendors will be asked to use less packaging material when they ship to us. All packing material used in shipments we receive will be reused, or provided to a vendor who reuses such material.
2. Recycling & paper use: Desktop & workstation recycling of materials is provided, including paper, glass, metal and plastic. Recycled paper will be used in all aquarium publications, or paper made from materials other than wood pulp. An ongoing commitment will be made to scale back paper consumption (reduced demand, two-sided copying, electronic forms for in-house ordering rather than paper forms).
3. Food service: Our exclusive food service vendor will be expected to minimize food waste in restaurant and banquet operations.
4. Desalination: Operation of an onsite desalination plant will supply water that flushes aquarium toilets (between 4 million and 5 million gallons/year). Use of City water will be minimized in a continuous effort to reduce water use. Water conservation helps protect native species in the Carmel River watershed on the perennially water-short Monterey Peninsula.

B. Alternative Transportation
Commuting alone by gasoline-powered automobile uses non-renewable resources, pollutes the air and ocean and contributes to congestion on city streets. Aquarium practices address all these issues by: providing free bus passes to commute to work; supporting a community visitor shuttle bus during peak summer months; offering parking subsidies for carpools and rideshares; charging solo commuters to park onsite; subsidizing an employee vanpool; offering payroll deduction for bicycle purchase. Alternative transportation use by employees will be actively promoted, monitored and recognized.

C. Hazardous Materials Handling
It is easier to improve environmental health by keeping toxins out of the system in the first place than to clean up pollution

afterward. Aquarium policies minimize the use of toxic materials and require proper disposal of those materials we use.

1. Purchase & use: The aquarium is committed to buying and using the least hazardous materials available that will do the job, to practicing integrated pest management, and to using non-toxic or least-toxic materials. We maintain an approved list of cleaning and disinfecting products, and all approved products are the least toxic that work effectively.
2. Disposal: The aquarium complies with all state and federal laws for safe disposal of hazardous materials.

D. Utilities
We are committed to conserving energy and water by reducing the power we use, and seeking out cost-competitive suppliers who generate energy with the fewest environmental impacts.

1. Source suppliers: We are committed to purchasing power for a cost-competitive rate from a supplier whose operations have minimal impacts on the environment.

2. Efficiency: We will conduct energy and water-use audits, and retrofit our fixtures and equipment to reduce consumption both of water and energy. These activities have already resulted in substantial cost savings, as well as conserving resources.

E. Seafood Awareness and Consumption
We're committed to making responsible decisions about seafood consumption, even though we recognize that it's often impossible to obtain all the information necessary for an informed decision. We base our seafood purchasing decisions on the best information available. We regularly seek out new scientific information, and we change our menu and our seafood buying practices whenever the data indicate. We share what we learn with others.

1. Food service: Our menu will reflect current information about sustainable fisheries. We inform visitors about what

we have done, and why. We will share our knowledge with other California tourism businesses and the public.

2. Husbandry operations: We have altered our seafood purchases for our living collection, and are committed to making additional changes as new information warrants.

F. Merchandise Operations

The merchandise we carry and the guidelines we provide to vendors are powerful tools for affecting public perception and changing the buying practices of our suppliers. We use these to promote conservation awareness, and we share what we do with colleagues.

1. Purchasing policy: We sell no products produced from living creatures if those products send an inappropriate message about the conservation of wildlife and ecosystems. We will not do business with vendors that manufacture, distribute or sell such products to other customers. We require direct or written documentation from our business partners and vendors regarding origin of living materials used in their products.

G. Environmentally Sensitive Purchasing and
Operations Practices

Business operations and buying decisions throughout the aquarium can have a positive environmental impact; can change public perception; and can help create markets for environmentally benign products and services.

1. Conservation mind-set during capital construction process: Planning for capital projects will include consideration of conservation impacts and design of conservation features into the projects.

2. Alternative fuel aquarium vehicles: We will analyze the possible purchase of alternative fuel vehicles every time we consider replacing or adding to the aquarium fleet.

3. Organic foods through our exclusive food service vendor: We will serve organic food products when they are cost-competitive with conventionally grown foods. To help

drive the market, we ask our food suppliers to actively seek out additional organic produce for purchase at cost-competitive prices.

4. Purchase of office supplies: We will encourage purchase of recycled products to create a market for recycling. We will provide staff with purchasing authority information about sources for recycled office supplies, and order only products with recycled content for communal office supply stocks.

5. Review and assessment of aquarium business practices: We seek to improve our business practices on a continual basis. We will encourage employees to find new and better products, or operating procedures that will conserve resources more effectively. We will consistently reward conservation-minded behavior through our employee recognition program. .

Permission granted by Ken Peterson, Communication Director

Components

GUIDING PRINCIPLE The environmental sustainability of your institution is a mission-based decision; implementation should come from mission-driven decisions on a daily basis. So what is your mission-related position on sustainability? The Madison Children's Museum has what it calls sustainability commitment: "we focus on children, including their future. We are committed to being a sustainable organization, balancing economic, social, and environmental factors to help ensure that we meet our present needs, while enabling future generations to meet their needs. We empower and equip children to actively shape the world they will inherit." Here is an adaptation of an idea from Piacentini: "We're going to operate [the museum] like we care about [the Bay/the Susquehanna River Watershed/the long-term protection of world heritage/species diversity]."

PURPOSE: WHY AND WHAT OMSI says that it "has adopted sustainability as a strategic value" and that it "tries to make its decisions based upon the triple bottom line of environmental, social, and fiscal responsibility." It focuses its sustainability efforts in four areas—large ones, but clearly identified areas—CO_2 emission reduction, waste reduction and prevention, exhibit production, and public education.[28]

Madison Children's Museum also defines four focus areas, but with a more generalized format: "As educational and community leaders, we will:

> ❖ integrate the principles of sustainability into all major business decisions
> ❖ seek strategic collaborations
> ❖ evaluate and reduce the environmental impacts of our operations
> ❖ design and develop our products, services, and materials with the long-term health of our children and community in mind"[29]

AUTHORITY, COMMITMENT, AND OVERSIGHT: WHO, HOW, AND SO ON Policy development and implementation require full participation by the board and staff leadership, with understanding of all staff ramifications. Developing this policy is not a one-person job; it is an institution's job—or it must be if it is going to work. OMSI's committee has a chair from senior management, and departmental participation from exhibits, programs, finance, human resources, maintenance, and sponsorship. Among other charges, its role is to:

> ❖ Serve as a central point of information and communication on issues and projects related to sustainability
> ❖ Identify projects that move us closer to performance targets and meet triple-bottom-line standards of success
> ❖ Prioritize and intensify activities throughout the organization
> ❖ Document and communicate progress within this area

Action plans implement policy. Your green team's action plan will be a significant part of the institution's sustainability action plan. This is where you should identify evaluation methods and goals. OMSI's work plan for fiscal year 2008 had these action steps:

> ❖ Propose for adoption performance targets for the organization's sustainability efforts
> ❖ Identify, research, and prioritize areas of greatest potential impact related to sustainability

> ❖ Advise senior management of these opportunities and propose a plan to address them
> ❖ Serve as a resource to accomplish projects approved by senior management
> ❖ Drive internal communication of progress and success
> ❖ Serve as a resource for emergent and cutting-edge sustainability issues

Your institution will have its own needs, culture, and environment to consider, and so you will create your own format for a policy. What is important is that you create the policy. Create it and attend to it as conditions evolve.

We said at the beginning that there are shades of green. Some of us will be less green than others will be, personally and professionally. So when you are faced with a decision, large or small, how will you decide how green to be? Some will say "we are going to be the greenest of the green." Some will use LEED criteria. Most will handle the questions case by case, using mission and policy as a guide.

The answer will not always be clear-cut, of course. So, as we said at the beginning of the first chapter, ask yourself: Does this green element positively affect institutional capacity, directly or indirectly? Does this green element positively affect mission-related public value, directly or indirectly?

If you answer yes to either question, then the green option becomes highly desirable. Increasing capacity often improves ability to fulfill mission, so a yes to the first question should encourage you to consider how much an element will increase capacity. Increasing public value within mission is our job anyway, so a yes to the second question makes green a very desirable option. When green satisfies both questions, all that is left to consider is "how soon can we do it?"

Notes

1. For this section, Mary Lou Krambeer provided our introduction to green teams and excellent advice others echoed.

2. Peggy F. Bartlett and Geoffrey W. Chase, eds., *Sustainability on Campus: Stories and Strategies for Change* (Cambridge, MA: MIT Press, 2004), p. 44.

3. We all recognize that corn plastic currently has negative effects on the environment, but many feel that the cradle-to-cradle effects are still better than nonrenewable, nondegrading fossil-fuel plastics cradle-to-cradle.

4. Sarah S. Brophy and Elizabeth Wylie, "The Greener Good: The Enviro-Active Museum," *Museum News*, January–February 2008. Washington, DC: American Association of Museums.

5. Xanterra, Sodetto, and Bon Apetit are just a few of the companies that are leading the way on this issue.

6. The Green Restaurant Association has a database of products, www.dine-green.com; and the Green Home online store offers products as well: dgs.green-home.com/products/institutional_sales/food_service/.

7. www.nytimes.com/2007/05/29/nyregion/29ink.html?_r=2&oref=slogin&oref =slogin, accessed December 16, 2007.

8. www.pittsburghkids.org//SmoothCMS/ContentObject/AB3752D2-9224-4A16-BCA5-7960EF0C8A9B.pdf, accessed December 10, 2007.

9. www.greenexhibits.org, accessed August 10, 2007.

10. William McDonough and Michael Braungart, *Cradle to Cradle: Remaking the Way We Make Things* (New York: North Point Press, 2002).

11. www.laminaceramics.com/news/061807.aspx.

12. www.gelighting.com/na/home_lighting/ask_us/faq_ballasts.htm, accessed December 3, 2007; and www.philips-usa.com, accessed December 19, 2007.

13. hypertextbook.com/facts/2003/WeiLiangMok.shtml, accessed December 18, 2007.

14. www.rinnai.us/Products/water_heaters/faq.aspx, accessed January 27, 2007.

15. This text was provided by Aaron Binkley, AIA LEED AP.

16. www.dallasnews.com/sharedcontent/dws/dn/latestnews/stories/110207 dnmetzoowaste.2b277b7.html, accessed December 16, 2007.

17. www.naturalgas.org/environment/technology.asp#fuelcells and www.phipps .conservatory.org/greencomp1.htm, accessed December 10, 2007.

18. www.lacma.org/info/TransformingProgress.aspx, accessed December 10, 2007.

19. www.chicagosolarpartnership.org/index.php?src=directory&view=sponsors &srctype=display&id=45, accessed December16, 2007.

20. www.masstech.org/IS/press/pr_7_5_06_massmoca.html, accessed December 10, 2007.

21. W. Eric Kluz, "Green Sanctuaries: Rehabilitating and Managing Historic Sacred Places and Landscapes in an Environmentally Responsible Manner," *Sacred Places*, Fall 2007, p. 18, www.sacredplaces.org/documents/PSPmagazine_Fall2007 .pdf, accessed December 20, 2007.

22. www.rpi.edu/~kilduff/Stormwater/permpaving1.pdf, accessed December 9, 2007.

23. www.ecofloridamag.com/archived/corkscrew_swamp.htm, accessed December 10, 2007.

24. Derived from remarks by Michael Furbish, Edgewater, Maryland, November 15, 2007.

25. "Working Knowledge: Going Green," *Museum Practice*, Museums Association, Spring 2006, p. 56.

26. Joe Matyas, "Keeping It Green," *Communiqué,* Association of Zoos and Aquariums, August 2002.

27. Solar Design Associates, "Review of Monthly Reports for Adirondack Museum Photovoltaic System Second Year of Operation," p. 4.

28. www.omsi.edu/info/pr/detail.cfm?prID=196A896D-65B3-DF53-A4DEB72B 2BD4A77A, accessed December 18, 2007.

29. www.madisonchildrensmuseum.org/about-mcm/sustainability-commitment, accessed December 10, 2007.

CASE:
Go Green in Food Service

Bonnie Paganis is general manager of food services at Shedd Aquarium in Chicago. Here is her story about greening the food service section of Shedd:

> Environmental stewardship is one of the biggest motivators to work here at Shedd. I grew up on a small farm in Illinois and was taught to live sustainably by my parents. Not because of all the fear of global warming or other current issues, as we did not hear about that then. It was because it made sense. We made a living from the earth so it was natural to take care of it. I have worked in food service my whole career and have sometimes been horrified by the negative impacts that some operations have on the environment. What a refreshing place to work, where the mission is to educate and connect guests to the living world.
>
> When I first started thinking about what we could do here, where to start, and what we could afford, I happened to attend a Green Festival in Madison, Wisconsin. The key speaker there was Alice Waters. She opened her speech talking about a meal she had at a museum and how horrible it was that fast food was served. She went on to say that she couldn't understand why those types of operations couldn't serve healthy, fresh food, especially as many of the guests were children. Of course that caught my attention! I got a chance to speak to her afterward and she gave me some good advice. Start slowly. Make one change at a time; make sure it is working; and then go on to the next. That was hard advice to take initially as I wanted to do things immediately.
>
> Well, the no-brainer for us was composting. Before we set up the pickup service, I hauled the compost home in a truck every week and used it on our farm. I was the garbage lady! The staff got used to putting the food scraps in a separate bin (really not hard) and we collected quite a bit. It was too much to keep hauling, so we decided that the program would probably work and we set up service with a local company. Now we call them when the green dumpster is full and they pick it up. The amount varies with business and time of year. The landscaping department also adds material.

The hardest challenge we have is sourcing compostable products as the companies do not seem to stay in business very long. But things seem to be getting better. I have set up with our equipment vendor to order cases in bulk and then deliver as I need them. They also put the Shedd logo on some of the items for us.

One of the most fun things I have done is the staff training. We do annual refresher training for the entire food service staff, which is now at ninety people. This year we had a green fair where we had booths for shade-grown organic coffee, Great Lakes conservation, vermi composting, sustainable seafood, and a few more things. The staff went from booth to booth and we had giveaways or raffles at each one. Then we split the staff into two groups and one went to the Wild Reef exhibit to hear about our Right Bite program among the animals it protects. The other group went to a Powerpoint presentation that I gave about waste management. Not a real racy topic, but we made it more interesting by going around the operation ahead of time taking pictures of all of them doing parts of their jobs that helped minimize waste. When I was taking the pictures they had no idea what I was doing so it was a surprise for them to see themselves on the screen. After talking about the three Rs [reduce, reuse, recycle], I flipped through the pictures and had them shout out which R the picture was an example of. Things like filling salt shakers, replenishing bulk condiments, separating trash, composting, etc. The fact that my staff is all "hams" made that a lot of fun.

Bonnie's approach includes excellent examples for starting your own green efforts:

- Leading by example: she started with herself (hauling waste home)
- Starting slowly: just one area (compost)
- Building up in-house until you pay for assistance: filling the green dumpster
- Providing training: so that the program is, and remains, truly effective
- Inviting participation: she used images of the team in action to promote training
- Providing a pleasant experience: enjoyable training, with encouragement, is far more effective than guilt

CASE:
Merging Green and Historic Preservation

At the President Lincoln and Soldiers' Home National Monument (a National Trust Historic Site), the renovation of the Robert H. Smith Visitor Education Center required LEED certification for uniting "sustainable planning policies with sustainable conservation treatments." The project is a snapshot of many sustainable practices compatible with historic sites (Figure 3.5). The renovation process used low-VOC products and recycled materials including carpet, countertops, wood, and flooring. Contractors separated materials for recycling and disposal, so metals, wood, masonry including concrete, cardboard, and general waste were monitored and separated. Implementing a segregated waste plan required that the construction management firm convince the subcontractors of the importance of recycling, require employee training, use bilingual signage, and exercise vigilance to execute the plan. Outside, the landscaping does not require irrigation and includes bioretention swales minimizing storm water runoff into the Potomac and the Chesapeake Bay. Inside, dual-flush toilets, automatic faucets, and automatic flush urinals reduce water use.

Of course the lovely, historic, tall windows with movable sashes contribute greatly to indoor air quality, bring in natural light, and help reduce the need for air-conditioning. Weather stripping was restored to improve energy efficiency. "We plan to *use* our windows," says David C. Overholt, preservation projects director. Reproduction period awnings moderate solar heat gain and are adjustable for the seasons. New energy efficient heating and air-conditioning was designed using energy modeling that helped predict what type of HVAC system was needed and what building improvements would help increase energy efficiency. The modeling helped the engineers "match the building envelope to energy expectations." The modeling indicated a need for increased insulation in some areas, and light-colored roof finishes to reflect exterior heat. The indoor air quality plan called for a makeup air unit in the attic that is working as expected, bringing in fresh air and capturing energy in the exhausted air to be recycled back into the building.

The building is being commissioned now and is expected to attain LEED Silver in 2008. Overholt points out that the commissioning agent represents the owner, not the builder. The agent is a

FIGURE 3.5. Look mom, the windows work! At the National Trust's President Lincoln and Soldiers' Home National Monument in Washington, DC, the renovation of the Robert H. Smith Visitor Education Center required LEED certification for uniting "sustainable planning policies with sustainable conservation treatments." The project is a snapshot of many sustainable practices compatible with historic sites. In our museums, and our homes, we have forgotten some very basic historical practices: rain barrels, shade trees, awnings, task lighting, daylighting, and windows that open. Preservation projects director David C. Overholt says, "We plan to *use* our windows." National Trust for Historic Preservation

third-party evaluator that helps the owner get what it paid for. "We've invested a lot of money in these systems and we want to know they're performing to expectations." Patrice Frey, director of sustainability research at the National Trust for Historic Preservation, says, "The LEED certification of the Lincoln Cottage Visitors Education Center is part of the Trust's Sustainability Initiative, which promotes the re-use of existing and historic buildings as inherently sustainable development." While there is a common perception that green building practices cannot be easily integrated with historic preservation projects, the Sustainability Initiative also seeks to demonstrate that historic preservation and green building practices are in fact complementary. The Visitors Education Center demonstrates the ease with which green building practices and historic preservation can be combined, and serves as a model for the sustainable rehabilitation of historic buildings.

The Money

THE TERM *environmentally advantaged* may sound a bit politically correct, but it is a powerful concept that gives institutions an edge in a competitive market for public attention and support. By integrating strategies for operational cost savings with mission objectives, museums are finding a powerful voice in green, one that is being heard and supported.

Fund-raising for green museums is less about finding green funders and more about finding funders who recognize, or are learning, that environmental sustainability is about long-term security and fulfilling your mission: conserving resources and saving money leaves more to support your mission-critical functions while contributing to the health, education, and well-being of your immediate and extended public.

This makes funding the development of a green project or building like funding any other museum project but with more opportunities for engaging the funder. So, special interest funders join those whose mission, audience, geographic focus, and programmatic interests match yours before you discovered sustainability. It is new and old together in your new prospect pool.

If you make your case clearly and confidently, the funders that support mission-matched organizations in thoughtful operations and capital projects will see environmental sustainability as institutional sustainability. There will be new funders who emphasize green building and practices regardless of your role as a museum, but they will neither displace nor replace your regular mission-specific funders who already provide capacity building and core support.

This means you still have to look for money everywhere all the time, only now with more prospects and more opportunities, we think the job is easier. Others do too. Stacy Nall, senior grants manager at the Children's Museum of Boston, says, "green is one of the easier areas to raise funds for." She feels that foundations and corporations are adopting green as an area of interest. Brooklyn Children's Museum president Carol Enseki says,

> [It] was much easier than we expected from a funding standpoint. We had tremendous enthusiasm among our stakeholders that helped carry it along. Private funders recognized that our project was more than just a building expansion, but a model project; one that demonstrated a commitment to addressing environmental issues, advancing innovation in design, and increasing public awareness about sustainable design. City, state and federal legislators recognized [that] our project supported their efforts and recent legislation promoting energy conservation.

Green brings more "new" with it than just prospects; it has new income vehicles and new opportunities. Payback and rebates are critical parts of the income package that other museum efforts do not offer. And the many new opportunities, products, and synergies offer you associated savings in resources and gains in partnerships. The cost is your learning curve, and the time spent creating alliances with funders and partnerships within your community. Follow the print and news media. Attend to which businesses and corporations are interested in green, which funders are adopting new areas of support, and what other nonprofits are headed in a similar direction. Prospecting and networking may be more promising than in the past as more organizations seek alignments with highly visible environmentally sustainable projects. So talk about what you are doing—sometimes a funder will find you. Many of the museums we encountered were not promoting their green aspects. Few had a green fact sheet outlining all that they were doing. Green is about institutional advancement. Including the public relations staff in your efforts can promote and educate simultaneously. Green is nothing to be shy about. It is the new mainstream and you do not want to miss out on that.

Sources and Approaches

Prospecting, Short Course

"Environmental sustainability" is not yet a search factor in the Foundation Center engine, but increasingly you will find "sustainability" and its variations in the funders' lists of interests or descriptions of grants awarded. But even if it were, you would still have to conduct triage on any funders interested in environmental sustainability to see if they were interested in your organization, mission, and programming.

So start with your mission and work from there. The model below, adapted from Abraham Maslow's hierarchy of needs satisfaction, is a useful way to assess the quality of the match between your project and a potential funder's interests. Start at the bottom of the pyramid and work your way up.

SARAH'S HIERARCHY OF FUNDER NEEDS (ADAPTED FROM MASLOW)[1]

Edge
Quality
Impact/Effect
Location and Audience
Organizational Mission

The three bottom rows of the pyramid are minimum criteria for any applicant-donor match: shared mission, audience targets, and geographic focus. They are also a match between your intended outcomes and the funders' goals for sustainability. If you can match up with a funder in those three areas, you are a promising applicant. Now consider the top two rows. Can you distinguish your organization from other applicants to survive the tough competition for private funding? Can you demonstrate a level of quality in your sustainable planning and performance that sets you apart from other applicants going green?

Environmental sustainability used to be the innovative or technical edge you could gain over others, but already it has dropped back to mere evidence of quality for some funders. The green arena is getting crowded. The trick is to identify what sustainable behaviors and opportunities distinguish your institution and your plans from all the other institutions going green. Your edge will be the synergy of your sustainable choices with your mission, operations, and location; the science and math behind your choices; and your project's ability to advance sustainability efforts in other institutions and communities.

Making the Case

Many museum staff say they do not know how to make the case for green in their art museum or history museum, or even why green aspects would interest funders at science and children's museums. They worry that if green is not the institution's mission, then asking for support of green is asking for support of mission creep. Or maybe the staff does not "do" green themselves and they feel hypocritical asking for something they do not really understand and they do not directly associate with the mission.

Let all of that go. For most museums, adding sustainability to the mix is a new level of institutional performance that requires all the same learning, adaptations, and growth that we experienced as a field dealing with other field-wide changes like Americans with Disabilities Act compliance and the shift from object-focused to visitor-focused. We are all learning a new language, adjusting our operations and policies, training our staff, and recognizing new visitors, funders, and partners.

Funders are adapting, too. The Merck Family Fund now asks invited applicants to describe their environmentally sustainable behaviors in their applications. This is not a criterion for funding, but an acknowledged learning opportunity for the funder. The fund invites applicants to measure their carbon footprint and to share ideas. It provides a climate change resource page, and indicates a strong preference for "organizations that have a commitment to recycled and reused products throughout their work" and for funding applications to be printed on double-sided, non-chlorine bleached, 100 percent recycled or alternative paper. (Alternative paper is nonwood or tree-free pulp made of garbage, hemp, agripulp, kenaf, bamboo, flax, cotton, and recovered cotton, for example. Green Seal sells varieties.[2])

Use math and science to help illustrate your case. Environmental sustainability is a powerful component of financial sustainability. Any green project or program that saves money is good for its bottom line and, therefore, contributes to its organizational sustainability. That is where the math comes in: be sure to include it in your case and the budget. If the project triggers payback over a longer term, be sure to explain the calculations and give examples of other similar successes.

For some readers, the science is the interesting part. Those focused on the money, but suspicious of myth-busting claims of money savings and affordability, will need the science and math of load reductions, air quality improvements, or waste transformation to get the full picture. The staff at the Boston Children's Museum, which opened its new building in 2007, feels that the LEED structure provides a standard many funders can understand and embrace—math and science. Not all funders will understand LEED yet, and all will need to know how LEED-related qualities affect your project, but be careful not to get so bogged down in the "what" and "how" during this part. Finish with the "why." Janet Anderson, associate director of EdVestors, a grant-facilitating agency in Boston, has a great saying: "At the end of your explanation, if I can still say 'so what?' then you haven't explained the outcome, the 'why.'" That's really your job as proposal writer. Use this opportunity to excite and engage the funder about the "so what" on your behalf.

Funding Examples

Probably the two best-known green funders for museums are the Kresge Foundation, which has become a leading funder of green building initiatives nationwide, and the Pittsburgh-based Heinz Endowments. Both funders made grants to the Senator John Heinz History Center in Pittsburgh and tied the awards to the building's green aspects: The Heinz Endowments funded the costs of documenting and obtaining LEED certification, while Kresge, which had already supported the planning process for the building, awarded a bonus grant when the center achieved LEED status. The Heinz Endowments in 2007 granted Phipps Conservatory and Botanical Gardens $100,000 in support of the design phase for its Living Building project to create what Phipps calls a "self-sustaining structure that eliminates the building's impact on the environment, including zero net-energy and water usage, and a contaminant-free, indoor environment."

The Kresge Foundation was an early supporter of the thoughtful planning that embraces green performance. The foundation aims to be a national nexus for philanthropic expertise, knowledge dissemination, and applied strategies for several of our society's most pressing issues. This includes addressing climate change through mitigation and adaptation strategies. "Through our Green Building Planning Grant program, we encourage people to make informed decisions about developing a high performance facility, which in essence is an environmentally sustainable building," says Sandra Ambrozy, senior program officer. "Since starting the program in 2003, the Foundation has awarded 119 planning grants totaling more than $7.4 million, including 16 grants to museums and cultural organizations."

In December 2005, the Jessie B. Cox Charitable Trust funded Clean Air Cool Planet for the Connecticut Science Center Collaborative, part of the New England Science Center Collaborative's mix of thirty science and nature centers, academic institutions, and state agencies, to identify the local impacts of and solutions to climate change in Connecticut, and provide educational content about the science of climate change linked to state science education frameworks. The Cox Trust, a regional trust, matched public funding and donations from in-state foundations such as the Tremaine Foundation. The trust makes grants in education, the environment, and health in New England. It provided $120,000 over two years to build the capacity of New England science centers to link climate change researchers and their discoveries to a public which at the time was largely unaware of the science behind the new concept.

Environment, not surprisingly, is connected to geography. The Heinz Endowments and the Jessie B. Cox Charitable Trust are geographically focused funders. You may find that other funders that focus geographically may begin to add categories that address environmental sustainability or articulate it as a competitive criterion. Those that have national or international interests are viable partners when you are working in collaboration with others for impacts of similar scope. Talk with potential funders as you plan your project to learn more about their opportunities in relation to yours, or to encourage them to consider environmental sustainability as a criterion. Perhaps your goal is to create a funding initiative; gather your non-profit colleagues and meet with funders around these mutual interests.

Agency Support: Federal, State, and Local

Federal support, and much state support, is still most common for projects involving innovative energy technologies, water quality and protection, and public education. EPA is an excellent resource for information, expertise, grants, loans, and compliance information. Start with the grants.gov site and remember you will have to register if you have never applied to the government before. You can also take an online training course before you apply for EPA funding. There are estuarial initiatives, storm water management, and agricultural programs that may be appropriate for you as a partner with others. For brownfield projects, EPA makes grants for assessments, revolving loan funds, and cleanup. You may be a perfect site for research by an EPA graduate fellow. EPA's environmental education grants support exhibits, programs, and activities in environmental education that increase public awareness and knowledge about environmental issues and provide the skills necessary to make informed decisions and take responsible actions. They are based on objective and scientifically sound information. They do not advocate a particular viewpoint or course of action. They teach individuals how to weigh various sides of an issue through critical thinking and enhance their own problem-solving and decision-making skills. The program must address health, community stewardship, education reform, career development, teaching skills, or capacity building.[3] It is no longer just the science of water, plants, and animals.

States participating in the federal government's Clean Energy Fund have grants for energy infrastructure. They may be your source for funding wind or solar power. Visit cleanenergystates.org to find out if your state is one of the eighteen with money for clean energy projects. Their goal is to expand markets for clean energy by funding infrastructure, so that is all they are interested in. If you can help them do that, then you are a viable candidate.

In New York, the New York State Energy Research and Development Authority gave the Adirondack Museum $118,000 for a photovoltaic system on the roof of its Special Exhibits Gallery. It also gave "approximately $250,000 towards the cost of the photovoltaic panels and energy analyses" to the Brooklyn Children's Museum, and the New York Power Authority gave $500,000 in financing for the geothermal heating system and other high-performance features. Since the city owns the Brooklyn Children's Museum building, it is saving itself some money: an estimated $103,000 per year in energy costs.[4]

The Dr. P. Phillips Orlando Performing Arts Center received $1 million from the Orlando Utilities Commission (OUC) for water and energy conservation. The center is in a major campaign and the OUC is interested in supporting its work as "one of the first major performing arts centers to achieve green certification" and as a leader "in energy and water efficiency."[5]

In Massachusetts, residents in towns using public utility services can buy green power. Those who do will earn credits for their town. The state provides a cash award in response. The town can use that fund for its own projects or for projects at nonprofit organizations, according to the wishes of the town. Now that is where your partnerships and alliances will serve you well, and your community.

When it comes to funding energy efficiency activities, your system or building design consultants should be proactive in helping to research applicable options. With the growth of sustainable design in all sectors and the rapid rise in energy costs, the funding landscape changes quickly and practitioners are more likely to know of these sources or where to check for them.

Nongrant Programs

When you begin your energy efficiency journey in an existing building, we hope you will start with an energy assessment. You may be able to arrange for an assessment through the local utility. The engineer doing the assessment should follow up with information on utility rebates and subsidies for appropriate energy efficiency measures. These programs are more likely to provide rebates than grants to ease paying for your new energy system, and of course the new system means you will reduce your energy costs.

In the Pacific Northwest, Puget Sound Energy's (PSE) grant programs provide about 50 percent of the cost to improve energy efficiency if you use electricity or natural gas. There are highly specific eligibility criteria, but nothing more complicated than a federal proposal. Missouri has an energy efficiency leveraged loan program. In Massachusetts, the Massachusetts Technology Collaborative's Renewable Energy Trust (MassTech) awarded MassMoCA a $700,000 Green Buildings and Infrastructures program grant for a 50-kilowatt solar installation, energy efficiency equipment, and an exhibit on the benefits of clean energy. Photovoltaic installations at Mass Audubon and The Trustees of Reservations have also been supported by MassTech. So call your state agency. Ask about funding, about what programs they think you may fit, and if they have suggestions for other programs where you might qualify for support.

For rebate programs funding energy production or efficient systems, pay attention to the timing of the award as you manage your cash flow, and whether the program guidelines truly match your project: payback period, equipment types and efficiency levels, energy types, and physical location. You know the process: read the guidelines and talk to the funders. They can guide you in applying. Programs probably cap individual award amounts and the totals awarded across the state. Often programs that look good at first glance are not actually open to nonprofits—only municipalities, corporations, and individual homeowners. Talking with the program managers, though, can help you sort through the bureaucracy and go directly to whichever programs are designed for your type of institution and project. As in any fund-raising project, creating a relationship with the donor is the first, most important step.

Some museums explore performance contracts with energy service companies (ESCOs). The arrangement provides energy efficiency assessments, equipment upgrades, and system changes that improve the energy performance of existing facilities. A performance contractor estimates potential energy cost savings for the museum, and the museum and contractor divide the amount saved. The more energy cost savings generated, the more the performance contractor earns—and the more money the museum has to put toward other projects. The formula for that division is negotiated prior to the lease signing.[6] As with any vendor, be sure you understand the terms, who will provide the actual service, and the trade-offs compared to in-house management or a consultation agreement. Create a relationship with the vendor that supports a shared understanding of institutional policies on energy efficiency. You want the vendor to make informed energy decisions based on your mission principles.

Corporate Support

Corporations embraced green long before nonprofits began considering it, but their funding for it is idiosyncratic. Support is commonly for sponsorships of programs, exhibits, or building components. The Home Depot Foundation sponsors the National Building Museum's lecture series For the Greener Good. The series is designed to create public discussion and debate, perhaps ideas and options, on topics associated with environmental sustainability and the myriad of public issues it connects with.[7] Carrier, a United Technologies Corporation company, supports the environment and sustainability including "green building practices and environmental sustainability in urban centers." It granted $55,000 to the National Trust for Historic Preservation for support of green building principles in the historic preservation project at the Visitors Education Center at the President Lincoln and Soldiers' Home in Washington, DC. And British Petroleum *did* pay $25 million for the naming rights to the photovoltaic-paneled grand entrance at the Los Angeles County Museum of Art.

Corporate funders may be interested in direct-impact community contributions through support of smart-growth practices, environmental activities such as watershed cleanups, and recycling. If the funder identifies possible types of support such as equipment or capital purchases, then composting equipment and bins, cardboard baler machines, even composting toilets (excellent for botanical gardens, large outdoor museums, and nature trails and centers but also inside your buildings) may qualify.

Greenwashing shows up in all areas; funding is no exception. How stringent do you choose to be? Often this is a very difficult decision, and it is certainly related to mission. Some institutions have struggled over the decisions about accepting significant donations from organizations engaging in specific practices. The grant is valuable, highly visible support of green exhibits or activities, yet the donor may continue unrepentant unsustainable practices back at the plant. As you consider your sustainable practices policy, consider what alignment you wish it to have with gift and investment policies.

Mixing Funders

As with other projects, you will need a mix of funder types for much of what you do. Siemens and the Commonwealth of Pennsylvania's Department of Environmental Protection funded the purchase and installation of the 5 kilowatt solid oxide fuel cell at Phipps Conservatory and Botanical Gardens. The Cleveland Zoo put together funding for staff support of a two-year initial recycling effort with grants from four private foundations, the local utilities, and a corporate foundation. All were Ohio based, and all the foundations listed "environmental" or "quality of environment" as areas of interest.

The Solar House 2005, the award-winning Virginia Tech entry in the 2005 Solar Decathlon on the National Mall, became an exhibit at the Science

Museum of Virginia, but it was a team effort. Moving a house is expensive even if it is built on wheels. Each house in the competition was required to be designed to travel by tractor trailer to the competition site. This means some portions of the house got folded to fit the highway lane width, but the arrangements for hauling a wide load made the whole project expensive. Once it reached Richmond, there was some assembly required. A fully functioning house as an exhibit means water and electric hookups, including a geothermal well. Siting is important to maximize sun exposure throughout the most productive days of the year, but the heat island effect of the parking lot location put extra demand on the HVAC systems. The Department of Energy, sponsors of the decathlon, supported the move and installation with a grant of $30,000 matched by the museum. Individual donors to the museum helped, as did the Virginia Department of Mines, Minerals and Energy, Energy Division. Richard Simmons Drilling contributed the cost of drilling the 500-foot well, and eight other organizations supported the move. Another hundred supporters contributed, cash and in-kind, to the construction of the house.

Programming, whether associated with building components or not, is a marvelous partnership opportunity with funders. At ECHO, one private

FIGURE 4.1. Vermont has been known for its green mountains since the 1760s and the state welcomed green initiatives very early in the movement. It is no surprise that ECHO Lake Aquarium and Science Center at the Leahy Center for Lake Champlain in Burlington, Vermont, was an early adopter of green. They have been doing this long enough that an early funder for an exhibit has returned to support greening the café operations, menu, solid waste management, and related exhibits and programming. © Curran Photography, 2006

foundation funded an exhibit about making personal choices and how these choices affect the health of Lake Champlain. Four years later the same foundation is supporting greening the café operations, menu, solid waste management, and related exhibits and programming (figure 4.1). This builds on the earlier grant for the exhibit on making choices; this time visitors participate by making real choices during their museum visit.

Knowing your donor and cultivating the relationship will help you capitalize on that interest and commitment. The Chesapeake Bay Trust funded the Chesapeake Bay Maritime Museum's (CBMM) public workshop on greening the nonprofit campus. From other projects the trust already was comfortable with the museum's leadership, capacity, and sustainability interests. Supporting an on-site workshop that included education for twenty additional nonprofits made excellent sense, so the two institutions worked together to create a highly effective, mission-satisfying project. The two-day program began with a day-long public how-to presentation and discussion by sustainability experts from the region. On the second day CBMM staff and consultants assessed the museum's campus and began sketching a multiyear action plan for implementing sustainable practice campuswide. The workshop gave the trust a chance to benefit twenty additional area nonprofits and helped the museum create a plan for sustainable practice and construction for its long-term efforts.

As always, the museums that are able to create a synergy among funders—private and public, local and broader ranging—will create strong partnerships that support the first project and the next projects. The National Oceanic and Atmospheric Administration (NOAA) and the Chesapeake Bay Trust are supporting construction of the living shoreline at CBMM. Where there have long been stand-alone vertical barriers at the water's edge, the museum will restore graduated wetlands that will absorb more of the water rise during high tides and storms. The new natural design will filter storm water runoff, add natural habitat, and provide an interpretive area where visitors will learn about natural bay processes and will be able to see at least a small portion of landscape that shaped the area's heritage. The best part of the story? It was NOAA's idea that CBMM apply for funding.

Green is that way. It is a motivator and a trigger for innovation. Most of the practices around environmental sustainability are still being refined and will be for awhile. Engaged funders with specific agendas may look to your institution to help them fulfill their goals. In Chicago, a new initiative started with the funders. Two local foundations—the Stearns Family Foundation and the Searle Funds of the Chicago Community Trust—recruited the Chicago Botanic Garden to work with the North Lawndale Employment Network, the Chicago Christian Industrial League, and the City Colleges of

Chicago on a project that will benefit residents of North Lawndale, an inner-city neighborhood that suffers from high rates of poverty, unemployment, and chronic disease associated with poor nutrition and deeply stressed living patterns. Low educational achievement, an adult incarceration rate greater than 50 percent, and routine drug-related violence define a community in struggle. The Chicago Botanic Garden is the lead institution in Windy City Harvest, a social enterprise that will provide job training and transitional employment for local residents through a year-round organic vegetable and plant production business on a recently acquired fifteen-acre site in North Lawndale.

According to Patsy Benveniste, vice president of community education programs at the garden, Windy City Harvest, which is a supporting organization of the garden, seeks to become sustainable as a green economy enterprise. Benveniste describes the developing project and site as "a training and community education center … that will use urban agriculture, nutrition education and green collar business as a bridge to schools, local organizations and individual residents—and as a catalyst for overall community development." Windy City Harvest will use the emerging green economy as a platform to establish local, sustainable food production, and in so doing will seek to help residents acquire marketable job skills that support the health and vitality of North Lawndale and the city of Chicago generally. The project hopes to develop a full menu of green collar activities including organic foods entrepreneurship, green roof plant evaluation and production, urban arboriculture, and soils testing and remediation.[8]

Individual Donors

Individual fund-raising will continue to be the greatest part of your institutional income and capital campaign support, but it will vary according to each institution's situation. People who are interested in environmental sustainability usually are not very passive about it. If they know what you are doing, they will identify themselves and work with you: ECHO's third-largest private gift came from a donor motivated by the green aspects of the project. They may come to you. That was the case at the Grand Rapids Art Museum (GRAM), because of what they were *not* doing. GRAM's idea for a new building did not include green. The Wege Foundation in Grand Rapids, Michigan, made a record-breaking $20 million gift—one-third of the building cost—predicated on the new GRAM being a green building. Donor Peter Wege said, "I hope it inspires other cultural organizations to follow." GRAM's director, once she and the trustees learned more about the concept, embraced environmental sustainability.[9]

Conclusion

Much of this is new territory for fund-raisers in museums. You can improve your awareness, develop a new vocabulary, and learn to recognize potential partnerships and project synergies by exploring the websites of veteran environmental funders. Here is just one example. The William and Flora Hewlett Foundation is known for its environmental sustainability work in the American West. The foundation's careful assessment of needs, interests, and successes has helped them create a very thorough and thoughtful description of program intent that encourages powerful partnerships and program development. The guidelines describe continued expectations in capacity building, and collaborative and consensus-building work all within program interest areas including their Environment Program. The site is a lovely illustration of the language, interests, and ethos of funding projects with environmental sustainability goals.

Notes

1. Sarah S. Brophy, "'Green' Money: The Funding Landscape for Museums Thinking about Going Green," *Philanthropy News Digest*, September 15, 2006.

2. www.greenseal.org/resources/reports/CGR=TreeFree.pdf, accessed December 14, 2007.

3. www.epa.gov/enviroed/pdf/grants_fs.pdf, accessed December 1, 2007.

4. www.brooklynkids.org/press/cap_expansion.asp?cap_ex=50, accessed December 1, 2007.

5. "OUC Donates $1M to the Performing Arts Center," *Orlando Business Journal*, November 14, 2007.

6. National Association of Energy Service Companies. A searchable database of services related to the evaluation, financing, and implementation of energy-efficient improvements. www.naesco.org.

7. www.nbm.org/Events/Calendar/greenergood/, accessed December 10, 2007.

8. Sarah Brophy and Elizabeth Wylie, "Greener Good," *Museum*, January–February 2008.

9. Fred A. Bernstein, "In Michigan, a Green Museum," *New York Times*, March 29, 2007.

Afterword

W E HAVE used two words here often: *journey* and *champion*. Going green is a journey, not a destination. One thing is clear, institutions on a green journey need a green champion. Feel free to be the leader. We hope you will. That is why we wrote this book.

We often hear another word: *but*. That is: "Yes, but"; "Okay, but." These phrases come up often along the green journey as you and your team sort through the best strategies for your particular issue, program, budget, and timeline. One example: staff asked the planners to create a green roof, *but* then the team needed to examine the options. Should it be extensive or intensive, publicly accessible or not? What programming function would it solve? What kind of ongoing maintenance is required? Do first costs justify the benefits?

But comes up because practicing environmental sustainability is complicated, evolving, and conditional. *Complication* comes from the omnipresence of the environment: one part affects another, and another, and another. That is why synergy (some call it *integration* just like nature's systems) is so important. *Evolving* comes from increased demand and improved ability to respond to that demand. Not only are there more solutions, but there are more choices within solutions. *Conditional* is because each museum, and each site, is different. Much of what you decide will depend upon your particular environment.

That is why it is so important to embrace the evolutionary process, and to share our knowledge and experience to help one another (not just among museums but in our local, regional, national, and global communities). The world is relearning sustainability at a very great pace. Global climate conditions demand a response by institutions that are here for the long haul, as museums are: to collect, preserve, and interpret *in perpetuity*.

When you look across your institution, using metrics to examine energy and water use, and your waste stream, start making connections between the environmental impact of your museum and the impact of your staff, your neighbors, your town, and your region. The collective impact hits home and the list of things to do to conserve, to collaborate with others, and to educate about what you are doing grows.

It is a long list. It is an important list. It can be overwhelming, but give yourself a break: no one knows it all. The field of environmental sustainability is expanding so rapidly, and new research is coming out so frequently, that no one person or institution is going to know it all. If we all share our knowledge and experience, we can all make progress. We have to; this may be one of the most important to-do lists in the museum field.

Resources

THIS RESOURCE list can help you get started. Take the time to educate yourself and to make choices about the methods best suited to your organization. Included here are a mix of books and articles, and lots of websites: informational sites; agency sites for technical assistance and financial support; consultants and contractors; and museum-related sites. Some are appropriate nationwide, while others are very regional.

Greening is a huge growth industry and there are many, many people and organizations doing good work for themselves or for others. All provide some good starting information online. We have listed some of the many we have discovered. We do not endorse any particular provider; we provide links for exploration purposes only. We realize we will have missed very talented and high-quality resources who simply were not on our radar or who we did not have room to include at the time of writing.

Chapter 1: The Idea

ARTICLES AND BOOKS

Bartlett, Peggy F., and Geoffrey W. Chase, eds. *Sustainability on Campus: Stories and Strategies for Change.* Cambridge, MA: MIT Press, 2004.

Brophy, Sarah S. "Board and Staff: Welcoming the Green Revolution in Your Museum," *Sustainable Nonprofits, The Foundation Center's Philanthropy News Digest.* Washington, DC: The Foundation Center, April 15, 2007. foundationcenter.org/pnd/tsn/tsn.jhtml?id=176400001.

Brophy, Sarah S., and Elizabeth Wylie. "The Greener Good: The Enviro-Active Museum," *Museum*, January–February 2008. Washington, DC: American Association of Museums.

Brophy, Sarah S., and Elizabeth Wylie. "It's Easy Being Green: Museums and the Green Movement," *Museum News*, September–October 2006. Washington, DC: American Association of Museums.

Creighton, Sarah. *Greening the Ivory Tower.* Cambridge, MA: MIT Press, 1998.

Gore, Al. *An Inconvenient Truth: The Planetary Emergency of Global Warming and What We Can Do About It.* Emmaus, PA: Rodale Books, 2006. See also www.climatecrisis.org, the official site of the documentary film.

Hawken, Paul. *Blessed Unrest: How the Largest Movement in the World Came into Being and Why No One Saw It Coming.* New York: Viking, 2007.

Hawken, Paul, Amory Lovins, and L. Hunter Lovins. *Natural Capitalism: Creating the Next Industrial Revolution.* Boston: Little, Brown, 1999.

McDonough, William, and Michael Braungart. *Cradle to Cradle.* New York: North Point Press, 2002.

Todd, Nancy Jack. *A Safe and Sustainable World: The Promise of Ecological Design.* Washington, DC: Island Press, 2005.

WEBSITES

The Association for the Advancement of Sustainability in Higher Education (AASHE)

AASHE is a member organization of colleges and universities working to advance sustainability in higher education.

www.aashe.org

The American College and University Presidents Climate Commitment (ACUPCC)

ACUPCC is a high-visibility effort to address global warming by garnering institutional commitments to neutralize greenhouse gas emissions, and to accelerate the research and educational efforts of higher education to equip society to restabilize the earth's climate.

www.presidentsclimatecommitment.org/

The Geraldine R. Dodge Foundation
Their Going Green Toolbox is informative
www.grdodge.org/green/toolbox/index.htm

The William and Flora Hewlett Foundation
The foundation commissions scholars, researchers, and others to conduct research of benefit to the foundation in furtherance of its direct charitable activities; there are a number of important and influential publications in the environmental area.
www.hewlett.org/Publications/

The Sustainable Endowments Institute
This nonprofit organization is engaged in research and education to advance sustainability in campus operations and endowment practices. Founded in 2005, the institute is a special project of Rockefeller Philanthropy Advisors.
www.endowmentinstitute.org/sustainability/

The Association of University Leaders for a Sustainable Future
This site lists campus sustainability programs with links to their websites, potentially useful resources for museums seeking to go green.
www.ulsf.org

The Museum Association of New York
MANY's Thinking Green Resource Page has useful information on current greening activities among museums.
www.manyonline.org/MANY-Article03.htm

The Dictionary of Sustainable Management
An open dictionary for business leaders and students of sustainability and business-related terms.
www.sustainabilitydictionary.com

Collections Care and Historic Preservation

ARTICLES AND BOOKS

Frey, Patrice. "Measuring Up: The Performance of Historic Buildings Under the LEED-NC Green Building Rating System." University of Pennsylvania, 2007. Master's Thesis. This is a marvelous paper that addresses LEED-NC credits for many aspects of historic properties. It is a must-read for anyone doing green historic preservation.
http://repository.upenn.edu/cgi/viewcontent.cgi?article=1076&context=hp_theses, accessed October 20, 2007

Henry, Michael C. "From the Outside In: Preventive Conservation, Sustainability and Environmental Management." *The Getty Conservation Institute Newsletter* 22, no. 1, 2007.
www.getty.edu/conservation/publications/newsletters/22_1/feature.html, accessed January 4, 2008

Wylie, Elizabeth. "Advancing Your Mission with a Green Message." *Sustainable Nonprofits, The Foundation Center's Philanthropy News Digest.* Washington, DC: The Foundation Center, April 15, 2007.
http://foundationcenter.org/pnd/tsn/tsn.jhtml?id=170300002

Faul-Zeitler, Roberta. "Green Museum Design: Is It Good for Collections?" *Collections: A Journal for Museum and Archives Professionals* 2, February 2006. Lanham, MD: Alta Mira Press.

"Special Issue on Sustainability and Preservation." *APT Bulletin, The Journal of Preservation Technology* 37, no. 4. Published by Association for Preservation Technology International, Albany, NY.
     www.apti.org

Appelbaum, Barbara. *Guide to Environmental Protection of Collections.* Madison, CT: Soundview Press, 1991. A revised version, featuring a section on green practices and collections care, is scheduled to be issued in 2009.

WEBSITES

From Gray Areas to Green Areas: Developing Sustainable Practices in Preservation Environments, November 1–2, 2007; organized by the Getty Conservation Institute and the Center for Sustainable Development and the School of Information's Kilgarlin Center for Preservation of the Cultural Record at the University of Texas, Austin. The conference website includes useful speaker bios and abstracts.
     www.ischool.utexas.edu/kilgarlin/gaga/index.html, accessed January 4, 2008

Association of Zoos and Aquariums Green Practices Scientific Advisory Group
     www.aza.org/RC/RC_Green/

The Greening of Historic Properties National Summit. Pittsburgh History and Landmarks Alliance and Green Building Alliance collaborated with the National Trust for Historic Preservation on this conference, a national forum on the greening of historic buildings. The website links to a conference white paper and briefing book with case studies and useful recommendations.
     www.gbapgh.org/Programs_PHBG.asp

Chapter 2: The Metrics

WEBSITES

Carbon Calculators
     www.carbonfootprint.com/
     www.climatecrisis.net/takeaction/carboncalculator/

www.nature.org/initiatives/climatechange/calculator/
www.epa.gov/climatechange/emissions/ind_calculator.html

Dartmouth College's Hood Museum of Art
Adaptation of the ECO Vermont Carbon Lite Checklist for office operations, and staff readiness.
www.dartmouth.edu/~sustain/resources/

The U.S. Green Building Council
This nonprofit originated the Leadership in Energy and Environmental Design (LEED) Program; their site offers a wealth of information.
www.usgbc.org

U.S. Department of Energy's Office of Energy Efficiency and Renewable Energy
The EERE site is a useful portal for a number of tools and metrics, case studies, and even curriculum plans.
www.eere.energy.gov/

Energy Star
A joint program of the U.S. Environmental Protection Agency and the U.S. Department of Energy.
www.energystar.gov/

Green Globes
This rating system offers an online assessment protocol, and guidance for green building design, operation, and management and provides market recognition of a building's environmental attributes through third-party verification.
www.greenglobes.com

Smith, Timothy. "Green Building Rating Systems: A Comparison of the LEED and Green Globes Systems in the US." Western Council of Industrial Workers, University of Minnesota, September 2006.
www.thegbi.org/assets/pdfs/Green_Building_Rating_UofM.pdf, accessed January 27, 2008

Waste Stream Audits

The New York State Association for Reduction, Reuse and Recycling, www.nysar3.org., in its business category has a great waste audit section.
www.nysar3.org/businesses/wasteaudit.htm.

Association of Vermont Recyclers
Tips on doing a waste audit or assessment, and forms to help.
www.vtrecyclers.org/wastekit/index.htm

Chapter 3: The Options

Green Teams

Association of Zoos and Aquariums
How to start a green team (wherever you are).
www.aza.org/RC/Documents/StartGreenTeam.pdf

New England Science Center Collaborative
Greening Your Science Center webpage
www.sciencecentercollaborative.org/greening.php

Reduce, Reuse, Recycle

California Integrated Waste Management Board
This site's Waste Prevention Information Exchange is a useful directory
of resources and information covering everything from appliances to
xeriscaping.
www.ciwmb.ca.gov/WPIE/

Earth 911
The zip code directory for recycling service centers for a broad range of
items is a valuable resource on this site that also offers green tips, news, and
articles.
earth911.org/

A Contractor's Waste Management Guide: Best Management Practices and
Tools for Job Site Recycling and Waste Reduction in Hawaii
An excellent guide with forms. Applicable outside Hawaii.
www.hawaii.gov/dbedt/info/energy/publications/cwmg.pdf

ECO-CELL
Cell phone recycling program for environmentally minded fund-raisers.
www.eco-cell.org

Fact Sheet for Restaurant Waste Reduction
North Carolina Department of the Environment and Natural Resources Division of Pollution Prevention and Environmental Assistance, October 1999
www.p2pays.org/ref%5C03/02790.pdf

Online Communities for Redistributing Noncollections Materials
www.freecycle.com and www.craigslist.com

Products and Sourcing

The Green Guide
Originated as a print newsletter in 1994, Green Guide was acquired by the National Geographic Society in March 2007; they have a useful product guide that outlines the environmental issues connected to products and then the environmentally friendly solutions including links to product manufacturers.
www.thegreenguide.com/

California Integrated Waste Management Board
This site offers a list of companies that manufacture products designed to degrade in the composting process.
www.ciwmb.ca.gov/FoodWaste/Compost/Biodegrade.htm

EcoProducts
This company headquartered in Boulder, Colorado, offers green products for food service and janitorial supplies.
www.ecoproducts.com

Dirtworks
This Vermont company provides biodegradable bags, mulch, cleaning liquids, pet supplies, and fertilizer.
www.dirtworks.net/

FlashBags
The vendor that ECHO uses to convert out-of-date exhibit banners into bags for their retail shop.
flashbagsonline.com/

Operations

Green Hotels Association
    This association encourages, promotes, and supports the greening of
the lodging industry, from adding "Drinking water served on request only"
to the menu to installing new HVAC systems, and every measure in between
to reduce operating costs as well as the hotel's impact on the environment.
    www.greenhotels.com

Coalition for Environmentally Responsible Conventions (CERC)
    This organization promotes environmental best practices for large con-
ventions, starting with the 2004 national political conventions in Boston and
New York, to establish a legacy of environmental, energy, water, transportation, and waste management best practices for future large meetings, urban
living, and commerce.
    www.cerc04.org/

Sheridan Associates/Sheila Sheridan
    Sustainable operations and facilities management consultant.
    sheilasheridan@comcast.net

Bon Appétit Management Company
    On-site custom restaurant company with a commitment to socially
responsible food sourcing and business practices, and strong partnerships
with respected conservation organizations.
    www.bamco.com

Sodexo
    Provider of integrated food and facilities management services in the
U.S., Canada, and Mexico. Their food services focus on local, organic, and
healthy ingredients grown through sustainable practices.
    http://www.sodexousa.com/usen/environments/leisure/leisure.asp

Xanterra Parks and Resorts
    Denver-based food service contractors at national and state parks
nationwide offer sustainable organic menu items and buy ingredients for
their park accounts from local farmers and growers.
    www.xanterra.com/environmental-action-364.html

Materials

Building Green
   Building Green is an independent publishing company that offers research and product information through *Environmental Building News,* a monthly newsletter, the GreenSpec directory of green products, and the Building Green Suite of online tools.
   www.buildinggreen.com

Oikos Green Building Source
   The site run by Iris Communications offers a product directory, a library of case studies, and a bookstore.
   oikos.com/

Cradle-to-Cradle product certification
   www.mbdc.com

Get Into Green
   The resource section of the National Building Museum's the Green House exhibit is a great source for materials and other good building information.
   www.nbm.org/Exhibits/greenHouse2/greenHouse.htm, accessed May 30, 2007

Exhibits and Materials

Madison Children's Museum sponsored site
   This site was launched to provide museum exhibit designers and fabricators a resource for designing and building exhibits and environments that best support healthy spaces and a healthier future for kids and the environment. Check out their cases and their sustainability guidelines for contractors.
   www.greenexhibits.org

University of California at Davis Design Museum
   Tim McNeil and his students pursue environmentally sustainable exhibit techniques.
   designmuseum.ucdavis.edu/index.html

Skyline Design

This exhibit design firm has shifted its museum exhibit program to sustainable "Greenplay" systems. Check out its Green Learning Environment Guidelines.

www.skydesign.com/greenplay/

Energy Efficiency

U.S. Department of Energy's Office of Energy Efficiency and Renewable Energy

The EERE site is a useful portal for a number of tools and metrics, case studies, and even curriculum plans.

www.eere.energy.gov/

Energy Star

A joint program of the U.S. Environmental Protection Agency and the U.S. Department of Energy.

www.energystar.gov/

A Consumer Guide to Buying Energy Efficient Products for the Home

This site includes energy-saving tips as well as "10 Bright Ideas for Community Outreach" with a draft article, letters, and fact sheets.

www.buyenergyefficient.org/

Alliance to Save Energy

Founded in 1977, the Alliance to Save Energy is a nonprofit coalition of business, government, environmental, and consumer leaders.

www.ase.org/

Union of Concerned Scientists

This site offers a science-based overview on energy efficiency including information on current policy initiatives.

www.ucsusa.org/clean_energy/energy_efficiency/

Turn off your computers

www.microsoft.com/smallbusiness/resources/technology/hardware/do_
you_need_to_turn_off_your_pc_at_night.mspx

Clean Energy and Heating and Cooling

Northeast Sustainable Energy Association

This member-based organization's website offers a user-friendly overview of clean energy options.

www.nesea.org/energy/info/

Massachusetts Technology Collaborative
Massachusetts' economic development agency for renewable energy, the innovation economy, and e-health.
www.mtpc.org

National Renewable Energy Laboratory
The National Renewable Energy Laboratory (NREL) is the nation's primary laboratory for renewable energy and energy efficiency research and development. Their website offers an overview of biomass, solar, wind, and geothermal energy sources as well as a resources section for students and teachers.
www.nrel.gov/

American Solar Energy Association
www.ases.org/

American Wind Energy Association
www.awea.org/

International Geothermal Heatpump Association
www.igshpa.okstate.edu/

Lighting

U.S. Department of Energy Office of Energy Efficiency and Renewable Energy
Efficient Lighting Strategies (December 2002). DOE/GO-102002-0787.
www.eere.energy.gov/buildings/info/documents/pdfs/26467.pdf

Philips Lighting sustainability worksheets for professionals
www.nam.lighting.philips.com/us/pro_lighting/register.php

Lighting Research Center at Rensselaer Polytechnic Institute
The world's leading university-based research and education organization devoted to lighting—from technologies to applications and energy use, from design to health and vision.
www.lrc.rpi.edu/

Illuminating Engineering Society of North America
Guides, books, and links to manufacturers' sites.
www.iesna.org

International Association of Lighting Designers
www.iald.org/home.asp

Building and Site

ARTICLES AND BOOKS

Matthiessen, Lisa Fay, and Peter Morris. "The Cost of Green Revisited 2007." Davis Langdon. www.davislangdon.com/USA/Research/ResearchFinder/ 2007-The-Cost-of-Green-Revisited/, accessed August 10, 2007

Gissen, David, ed. *Big and Green: Toward Sustainable Architecture in the 21st Century.* Princeton, NJ: Princeton Architectural Press and National Building Museum, 2002. Accompanied an exhibition at the National Building Museum, January 17–June 22, 2003.

Brown, David, Mindy Fox, and Mary Rickel Pelletier, eds. *Sustainable Architecture White Papers.* New York: Earth Pledge Foundation, 2001.

WEBSITES

The National Park Service's Denver Resource Center publication *Guiding Principles of Sustainable Design,* particularly chapter 6, "Building Design."
   www.nps.gov/dsc/d_publications/d_1_gpsd_6_ch6.htm, accessed October 20, 2007

American Institute of Architects
   The website for this professional organization is very informative with a useful section on Architects and the Public and a download of the publication "You and Your Architect"; under Environment/Sustainability is a link to "How to Write a Green RFP."
   www.aia.org

The GreenRoundtable
   An independent nonprofit organization whose mission is to promote and support healthy, efficient, and sustaining development and building projects through strategic outreach, education, policy advocacy, and technical assistance. The GRT strives to mainstream green and ultimately become obsolete.
   www.GreenRoundtable.org

The Northeast England Sustainable Energy Association (NESEA)
A nonprofit organization to facilitate the widespread adoption and use of sustainable energy by providing support to industry professionals and by educating and motivating consumers to learn about, ask for, and adopt sustainable energy and green building practices.
www.nesea.org

Rocky Mountain Institute
An entrepreneurial nonprofit organization that fosters the efficient and restorative use of resources to make the world secure, just, prosperous, and life-sustaining, by inspiring business, civil society, and government to design integrative solutions that create true wealth.
www.rmi.org

The Leonardo Academy
A nonprofit started in 1997 to advance sustainability and distribute guidance, metrics, standards, education, and information to increase sustainability and make it practical for companies, organizations, families, and individuals.
www.leonardoacademy.org

The Vermont Green Building Network (VGBN)
The VGBN is a nonprofit networking organization dedicated to expanding the market for green building. The philosophy of green building promotes resource conservation, including energy efficiency, renewable energy, and water conservation. Green buildings are designed to take into account environmental impacts and waste minimization. They create a healthy and comfortable indoor environment, reduce operation and maintenance costs, and address issues such as historical preservation and access to public transportation and other community infrastructure.
vgbn.org/

The Center for Sustainable Building Research (CSBR)
Established as an official unit within the University of Minnesota College of Design (formerly known as the College of Architecture and Landscape Architecture) in 2001, although the staff has been conducting building research since 1997 in the following areas: sustainable design, energy efficient buildings, windows and glazing research, building design process and evaluation, human factors, and building science.
www.csbr.umn.edu

Centre for Alternative Technology (CAT)
CAT is concerned with the search for globally sustainable, whole, and ecologically sound technologies and ways of life. They have a free information service online and via phone.
www.cat.org.uk

Center for Sustainable Development
Its mission is to facilitate the study and practice of sustainable design, planning, and development in Texas, the nation, and the world through complementary programs of research, education, and community outreach.
www.utcsd.org/

Facilities Management

International Association of Museum Facilities Administrators
This group has an informative newsletter, *Papyrus*, and produces an annual benchmarking study.
www.iamfa.org/

International Facilities Management Association
Asset Lifecycle Model for Total Cost of Ownership Management: Framework, Glossary and Definitions
www.ifma.org/tools/research/Asset_Lifecyle_Model.pdf

International Facilities Management Association Foundation
Deliver the Green—A fresh look at LEED-EB and facility management.
www.ifmafoundation.org/deliverthegreen.pdf

Landscape, Storm Water, and Water Harvesting

Sustainable Sites
The Sustainable Sites Initiative is an interdisciplinary partnership between the American Society of Landscape Architects, the Lady Bird Johnson Wildflower Center, the United States Botanic Garden and a diverse group of stakeholder organizations to develop guidelines and standards for landscape sustainability.
www.sustainablesites.org/

American Society of Landscape Architects
Sustainable Design and Development Professional Practice Network is a group committed to ecology-based planning and design; creating land-

scapes that balance the needs of man and the environment while benefiting both. Their website and newsletter are useful resources.
host.asla.org/groups/sddpigroup/

Stormwater Authority
A resource for information, news, events, and education on storm water, the site includes a state-by-state guide to regulations and best practices.
www.stormwaterauthority.org

The Texas Manual on Rainwater Harvesting
A highly regarded publication about rainwater harvesting.
www.twdb.state.tx.us/publications/reports/RainwaterHarvestingManual _3rdedition.pdf

Chesapeake Ecology Center
Guide to xeriscaping, rain gardens, and conservation landscaping.
www.chesapeakeecologycenter.org/images/primer_lowrez1206_2.pdf

Florida Green Industries
Publication, "Best Management Practices for Protection of Water Resources in Florida." Useful for indoctrination into topics of runoff, turf management, irrigation systems, design and installation, fertilizing, and pest control.
www.dep.state.fl.us/central/Home/MeetingsTraining/FLGreen/FLGreenI ndustries.htm

Plant Conservation Alliance
Very rich information resource including lists of native plants for habitat and conservation landscaping, by region.
www.nps.gov/plants/

Rain Gardens and Permeable Paving Systems (images and definitions)
www.seattle.gov/dpd/static/GF_RainGardens_1_37427_DPDP_019875 .pdf

Hot Water

Rinnai Tankless Water Heaters
www.rinnai.us/

Viessman High-Efficiency Boilers
www.viessmann-us.com

Green Roofs

Emory Knoll Farms
www.greenroofplants.com/, accessed November 30, 2007

Green Roofs for Healthy Cities
This is a nonprofit industry association promoting the industry throughout North America. Its mission is to increase the awareness of the economic, social, and environmental benefits of green roof infrastructure across North America and rapidly advance the development of the market for green roof products and services. It is a resource for meetings, training, products, services, and great reports and information.
www.greenroofs.org

Peggy Notebaert Museum Nature Museum, Chicago, IL.
Public education material on green roofs.
www.naturemuseum.org/greenroof/planningaroof.html, accessed October 22, 2007

Michigan State University's green roof information www.hrt.msu.edu/faculty/Rowe/Green_roof.htm, accessed October 22, 2007

Programming

EE-Link Environmental Education on the Internet
A vast repository of links to resources, sponsored by the North American Association for Environmental Education.
eelink.net

An Inconvenient Truth, the documentary film's website
www.climatecrisis.net

Conservation Messages
These conservation messages were developed by the Conservation Education Committee of the American Zoo and Aquarium Association and are recommended by CEC as appropriate to the conservation education missions of AZA zoos and aquariums.
www.aza.org/ConEd/ConMessages/

Alliance to Save Energy
This organization's Kids' Page offers environmental info and news and links to other kids' energy websites.
www.ase.org/section/_audience/consumers/kids/

Edutopia: The George Lucas Educational Foundation
This Go Green Database is a directory you can search by topic, grade level, cost, or location to inform programming to engage children in environmental awareness.
www.edutopia.org/go-green

GreenMuseum
Nonprofit, online museum of environmental art.
www.greenmuseum.org

Chapter 4: The Money

ARTICLES AND BOOKS

Brophy, Sarah S. "'Green' Money: The Funding Landscape for Museums Thinking about Going Green." *Sustainable Nonprofits, Philanthropy News Digest*, September 13, 2006. Washington, DC: The Foundation Center. foundationcenter.org/pnd/tsn/tsn.jhtml?id=156500003

WEBSITES

Sarah S. Brophy, bMuse
Green team management and fund-raising support for museums and cultural nonprofits pursuing environmental sustainability.
www.bmuse.net

The Clean Energy States Alliance (CESA)
CESA is a nonprofit organization composed of members from sixteen clean energy funds and two state agencies; it provides information and technical services to its members and works with them to build and expand clean energy markets in the United States.
www.cleanenergyfunds.org/about.html

Database of State Incentives for Renewable Energy (DSIRE)
A source of information on state, local, utility, and selected federal incentives that promote renewable energy. DSIRE is an ongoing project of the Interstate Renewable Energy Council (IREC), funded by the U.S. Department of Energy and managed by the North Carolina Solar Center.
www.dsireusa.org

Environmental Grantmakers Association

The Environmental Grantmakers Association (EGA), a project of the Rockefeller Family Fund, was formed in 1987. Today, members represent over 250 foundations from North America and around the world.

www.ega.org

The Funders' Network for Smart Growth and Livable Communities

The mission of the Funders' Network is to strengthen and expand funders' abilities to support organizations working to build more livable communities through smarter growth policies and practices.

www.fundersnetwork.org

The Kresge Foundation Green Building Initiative

The initiative's Planning Grant program encourages nonprofits working in the arts, health, and human service areas to consider green for the first time. Planning grants are available in amounts from $25,000 to $100,000.

www.kresge.org

Massachusetts Technology Collaborative/Renewable Energy Trust

This state-funded effort offers funding for renewable energy applications; their database of case studies shows performance data on their funded projects and links directly to the Department of Energy's High Performance Buildings Database.

www.masstech.org

New Millennium Development

Programs and services to expand the market demand for zero-waste technologies, particularly those utilizing rapidly renewable resources and waste by-products. NMD goals are to educate, enable, and empower multiple industry sectors one community at a time by providing high-impact learning experiences.

www.newmillennium.us

Architects, Landscape Architects, and Engineers

The building and landscape projects that we mention in the book are largely the result of integrated teams of designers, engineers, and owners all working toward a common sustainable goal. There are many fine professionals working across the country and we would urge you to check the list of

LEED-accredited professionals, your local USGBC and American Institute of Architects affiliates, and ask colleagues about good working experiences. We are not endorsing but are acknowledging the firms involved in the projects we cite as a way to underscore the importance of designers and technical experts in driving forward sustainable building and landscape practices. We apologize for not including everyone and salute all the creative and committed team members who are playing a vital part in greening museums.

Samuel Anderson Architects
www.samuelanderson.com

Architectural Design Inc.
www.ad-archts.com

Architectural Energy Corporation
www.archenergy.com

Astorino
www.astorino.com

Atelier Dreiseitl
www.dreiseitl.de

Beals and Thomas Inc.
www.bealsandthomas.com

BKSK Architects
www.bkskarch.com

Coastal Engineering
www.ceccapecod.com

The Collaborative Engineers
www.collaborativeengineers.com

Conservation Design Forum
www.cdfinc.com

Energy Balance, Inc.
andy@energybalance.net

Goody Clancy
www.goodyclancy.com

The Green Engineer
www.greenengineer.com

GroSolar (formerly Global Resource Options)
grosolar.com

Heritage Landscapes
www.heritagelandscapes.com

The Hickory Consortium
www.hickoryconsortium.org

HKT Architects
www.hktarchitects.com

Horiuchi Solien Landscape Architects
www.horiuchisolien.com

IKM Incorporated
www.ikminc.com

Integrative Design
www.integrativedesign.net

Carol R. Johnson Associates
www.crja.com

H. Keith Wagner Partnership
www.hkw-p.com

Koning Eizenberg Architecture
www.kearch.com

Lucchesi Galati Architects
www.lgainc.com

Machado and Silvetti Associates
www.machado-silvetti.com

Murase Associates
    www.murase.com

Nitsch Engineering
    www.nitscheng.com

Ove Arup and Partners
    www.arup.com

Perkins Eastman Architects
    www.perkinseastman.com

Perkins and Will
    www.perkinswill.com

Polshek Partnership
    www.polshek.com

Renzo Piano Building Workshop
    rpbw.r.ui-pro.com

RMJM Hillier (formerly Hillier Architecture Preservation Studio)
    www.hillier.com

SAS Architects
    www.sasarchitects.com

Solar Design Associates
    www.solardesign.com

Solar Works
    www.solar-works.com

Rafael Vinoly
    www.rvapc.com

Weiss/Manfredi Architecture/Landscape/Urbanism
    www.weissmanfredi.com

wHY Architecture
    www.why-architecture.com

Steven Winter Associates, Inc.
www.swinter.com

Zimmer Gunsul Frasca Partnership
www.zgf.com

Abbreviations

AAM	American Association of Museums
AARFAM	Abby Aldrich Rockefeller Folk Art Museum
APT	Association of Preservation Technology
ASHRAE	American Society of Heating, Refrigerating and Air-Conditioning Engineers
ASTC	Association of Science and Technology Centers
AZA	American Zoological Association
BCM	Brooklyn Children's Museum
BOMA	Building Owners and Managers Association
BREEAM	Building Research Establishment's Environmental Assessment Method (United Kingdom)
CAM	California Association of Museums
CAS	California Academy of Sciences
CBMM	Chesapeake Bay Maritime Museum
CFL	compact fluorescent lamp or light
CITES	Convention on International Trade in Endangered Species
CWF	Colonial Williamsburg Foundation
DCC	Doyle Conservation Center
DOE	Department of Energy
DSIRE	Database of States Incentives for Renewable Energy
ECHO	ECHO Lake Aquarium and Science Center at the Leahy Center for Lake Champlain
EPA	Environmental Protection Agency
EPBD	Energy Performance of Buildings Directive (European Union)
ESA	Endangered Species Act

ESCO	energy service company
GBI	Green Building Initiative
GG	Green Globes
GRAM	Grand Rapids Art Museum
HVAC	heating, ventilating, and air conditioning
IAMFA	International Association of Museum Facilities Administrators
ICLEI	International Council for Local Environmental Initiatives
IFMA	International Facilities Managers Association
IGLO	International Action on Global Warming
IPM	integrated pest management
LACMA	Los Angeles County Museum of Art
LCA	life cycle analysis
LCC	life cycle costs
LED	light-emitting diodes
LEED	Leadership in Energy and Environmental Design
LEED-EB	LEED for Existing Buildings
LEED-NC	LEED for New Construction
MAAM	Mid-Atlantic Association of Museums
MassMoCA	Massachusetts Museum of Contemporary Art
MBAq	Monterey Bay Aquarium
MCM	Madison Children's Museum
NAI	National Association of Interpreters
NEAq	New England Aquarium
NEMA	New England Association of Museums
NESCC	New England Science Centers Consortium
NOAA	National Oceanic and Atmospheric Administration
NPS	National Park Service
NYS3R	New York State Association for Reduction, Reuse and Recycling
NYSERDA	New York State Energy Research and Development Authority
OMSI	Oregon Museum of Science
PV	photovoltaic
QBG	Queens Botanical Garden
ROI	return on investment
SAG	Scientific Advisory Group
SAM	Seattle Art Museum
TBL	triple bottom line
USGBC	United States Green Building Council
VFD	variable frequency drive
VOC	volatile organic compounds

Glossary

aerators: Add-ons to faucets in sinks and showers that incorporate air into the water as it comes out. This reduces water consumption while providing a wider spray, and equal force.

ASHRAE 90.1: The American Society of Heating, Refrigerating and Air-Conditioning Engineers' guideline for evaluating the energy demands and costs of the heating, cooling, lighting, and other systems of the proposed design and comparing that to the comparable figures for a base building design that meets ASHRAE 90.1 prescriptive requirements.[1]

ballast: Fluorescent and compact fluorescent light bulbs use electronic, electromagnetic (hybrids), or magnetic ballasts. Their job is to start and manage the electricity flow into the lightbulbs. Electronic ballasts change the electric frequency, normally 60 hertz to a more efficient level of about 25 kilohertz. This uses energy more efficiently. Electronic ballasts for dimming fluorescent fixtures are relatively new to the market.

biodegradable: Able to break down completely and naturally into safe materials for the environment.

biofiltration: Using living materials, usually plants, to filter water.

biomass: A collective term referring to something previously living that is being converted into something else. Most often this means agricultural waste burned for heat or converted into energy.

biomimicry: Practices developed by studying and imitating nature's designs and processes. It is taken from the words *bios*, meaning life, and *mimesis*, meaning imitate. An example is high-rise architecture without air conditioning inspired by the ventilation systems in termite dens.

bioswale: Landscaped areas capture water runoff, retaining and cleansing it of silt and pollution before it is released into the storm sewer or watershed.

black water: Waste water from toilets and other contaminated uses that must be treated before discharge or reuse. Some organizations clean the black water onsite through living machines that are vegetated cleaning systems.

carbon footprint: Generally understood to be "a measure of the impact human activities have on the environment in terms of the amount of greenhouse gases produced, measured in units of carbon dioxide."

cardboard baler: A machine that will compress and tie cardboard into bales for purchase by recycling vendors.

commissioning: Building commissioning is the systemic process of assessing the building system design and postoccupancy performance compared to the design intent. In short, it makes sure the client gets the performance it asked and paid for.

compact fluorescent lights (CFLs): Those corkscrew-shaped lights that can be used in traditional light fixtures yet use significantly less energy. Note: they must be recycled properly because they contain small amounts of mercury that should be disposed of in a way that captures and recycles the mercury, preventing it from reaching waterways.

composting toilet: A toilet that uses the composting process to convert human waste into organic compost usable as a planting medium, and completely clean and safe.

credit: Often a tax credit, given to organizations or individuals installing and using an alternative energy system.

Database of States Incentives for Renewable Energy (DSIRE): An online listing, by state, of all renewable energy rebates and other financial incentives.

daylight harvesting: Allowing daylight to penetrate into buildings to reduce the need for artificial light.

daylighting: Using daylight to provide light inside a building, through windows, tubular devices, skylights, and wall placement; often called daylight harvesting. It is usually paired with light sensors so that as daylight conditions change, interior lighting conditions adjust.

eco-solvent: Low-toxin, low-petroleum solvents in inks that evaporate and leave behind the ink print.

energy audit: A review of energy use, including rates, amounts, types, fixtures, and demand levels to create benchmarks and locate areas for energy conservation or system changes.

energy service companies (ESCOs): Businesses that provide audits of building or whole-campus energy consumption and recommend a comprehensive suite of energy-saving measures. The ESCO is typically paid for the cost of the improvements through a guarantee of energy savings from the retrofits with a guaranteed level of energy savings.

Energy Star: A joint program of the U.S. Environmental Protection Agency and the U.S. Department of Energy. It is a combination of programs, tools, and products that help individuals and businesses save energy. Most people recognize it as the seal of energy efficiency on home appliances, but it is a larger program that includes online tools for calculating energy efficiency.

environmental sustainability: Practices that rely on renewable or reusable materials and processes that are green or environmentally benign (we think of that as "do no harm and keep the patient alive"). Many also use the definition of providing for our needs today in a way that does not limit the ability of future generations to meet their needs.

e-waste: Electronic waste like cell phones, computers and screens, PDAs, and so on.

extensive green roof: A green roof that is primarily a single shallow depth, with low-maintenance, low-growing plants.

geothermal: Existing heat inside the earth. Sometimes it comes out in hot springs; usually we access it through wells and pipes containing air or water at a nearly constant temperature of 55°F. In the summer this air or water is much cooler than outside air we would normally spend energy to cool to make our indoor temperatures more comfortable. Using air or water at cooler temperatures reduces the amount of energy we spend artificially cooling air. Conversely, the air or water is much warmer than outside air in the wintertime, reducing the degrees of heating required to reach a comfortable level indoors in winter. The system can use horizontal or vertical piping, water or air, and each choice affects the type of heat exchange system required to modify air temperature in the building.

gray water: Waste water from sinks, not contaminated but nonpotable; often reused to flush toilets.

green: In this book we use the term *green* to suggest or describe the array of environmentally thoughtful practices in museums. *Green* refers to products and behaviors that are environmentally benign (we think of it as the "do no harm" clause). Green is today's generic term for environmentally better practice.

Green Globes: An environmental assessment and rating system that was developed by the Green Building Initiative and grew out of the UK's Building Research Establishment's Environmental Assessment Method.

green roof: A roof, flat or sloped, built and planted to capture precipitation, clean it, and slowly release it into the air or into storage systems. They have the advantage of also reducing heat island effects. In some climates they provide substantial insulating value.

green team: A group of staff, volunteers, and often consultants, who work to research, implement, and evaluate the adaptation of green practices in the organization.

green wall: A planted vertical surface, either interior or exterior; also called a living wall.

greenwashing: Adapted from whitewashing, means exaggerating green properties or arbitrarily selecting the green aspects and ignoring the non-green aspects. The promoter may not take care to research or explain the extent of green, or will simply gloss over the data to capture the marketing appeal of green.

harvesting: Collecting something for use or reuse. You can harvest stormwater by collecting it from roofs and parking areas, and clean it and send it back to the waterways, or use it to flush toilets, wash vehicles, and irrigate landscape. You can harvest daylight by encouraging it to reach into the building to reduce artificial lighting.

heat island effect: The buildup of heat, in urban or built areas, as the sun's heat is absorbed in dark roofs and pavement. Heat island temperatures can differ dramatically from nearby suburban areas, or areas with green roofs, surface landscaping, and permeable surfaces.

impermeable surface: Any surface, often a roof or traffic area, that does not allow water to filter through.

integrated pest management (IPM): Using knowledge of pest life cycles and habits, along with environmentally sensitive practices, to control or eliminate pests.

intensive green roof: Often built with deeper growing medium, and holding more substantial plants and trees, often requiring more maintenance, as if in a park setting.

Leadership in Energy and Environmental Design (LEED): The LEED rating system was introduced in 2000 to provide a widely understandable and technically specific system for ranking levels of sustainability in buildings and operations. It is now an established brand and market force.

LEED AP: A voluntary professional certification earned by examination through USGBC. It guarantees the museum that the engineer or other consultant has passed the exam for competency in energy efficiency and sustainable building practices. It addresses the building and site issues primarily. The USGBC website lists LEED AP professionals.

LEED-EB: LEED for Existing Buildings.

LEED-NC: LEED for New Construction.

life cycle analysis: Analyzing the costs and environmental impacts of a product or service over its life span.

life cycle costs: All the costs associated with a product or service over its life span, including sourcing, producing, purchasing, running, and disposing of it.

living shoreline: A shoreline rebuilt to withstand tidal and wave action erosion that includes a mix of sloping barriers and reestablished natural vegetation and shoreline.

living wall: Vertical surfaces constructed to hold plants. The plants can improve indoor air quality and clean water if attached to appropriate systems. They can even be used for urban agriculture.

localvore: Someone who eats food produced locally in order to reduce the amount of transportation, and therefore pollution, required to bring food to consumers (and to encourage local farm and food economy).

make-up air: Fresh air drawn into a building to refresh air quality.

off-gassing: Gasses released from products: formed wood, carpeting, paints, adhesives, fabrics, and cleaning products, manufactured with chemicals that release gases and chemicals into the air after installation or use.

payback: The point where the cost savings or income generated from an item or system equals the cost to purchase and install the item or system (the first cost).

permeable surface: Any surface, often landscaping, that allows absorption of water.

phantom loads: Electricity from electronic items left plugged in that draw energy in their stand-by or off mode.

photovoltaics: Devices that convert sunlight into electricity. Most often found as solar panels, but also available as roofing shingles, and increasingly associated with portable and remote electrical appliances: cell phone chargers, pathway lighting, even stoves.

Portfolio Manager: An Energy Star online energy management tool that allows you to track and assess energy and water consumption across your entire portfolio of buildings in a secure online environment.[4]

radiant heating: Radiant heating systems involve supplying heat directly to the floor or to panels in the wall or ceiling of a space or building. It is also called infrared radiation. It is more energy efficient to heat the people, plants, animals, or objects than the entire space.

rain barrel: Barrels placed at the end of downspouts and rain chains, or other areas where rainwater runs off a roof, that catch and hold the water for reuse later in gardens. By capturing the water and preventing its discharge into the stormwater system, you achieve multiple goals: reusing the water, using plants and soil to clean it naturally, then sending it to recharge the groundwater system, thereby reducing stormwater management and treatment by the municipality, while simultaneously reducing the demand for energy and cost of using treated municipal water on gardens where nontreated is better for the plants. There are many types of rain barrels and systems to manage overflow, facilitate drip hose uses, and prevent mosquito breeding.

rain chain: A chain placed where a downspout would be, to direct the roof runoff to the ground or rain barrel and distribute it in a way that reduces erosion force when it reaches the ground.

rain garden: Gardens designed and placed to capture and then absorb rainwater runoff. Their filtering action cleans the water runoff and either distributes it to storm drains, nearby streams, or wetlands, or lets it recharge groundwater. Its plant materials can survive in periods of uneven moisture levels.

rebate: Money awarded to you through a formal program after a system has been installed and inspected. This is usually an alternative energy system, and the rebate is made by utility or an agency interested in promoting investment and use of the systems.

recyclable/recycle: Able to be transformed into something else—either another version of itself, or into another usable material.

renewable: A resource that regenerates or somehow replaces or repeats itself, preferably rapidly. Wind and sun are renewable because they continue to be available even as we use them. Bamboo is a rapidly renewable resource because it grows quickly and spreads widely—there is an easily renewable supply.

renewable energy: Energy from sources that do not deplete natural resources, but use natural resources that are renewed or replaced rapidly, such as wind, sun, geothermal heat, and biomass.

smart lighting: Systems that shut off when a room is unoccupied, or dim with available daylight, to reduce energy consumption.

solar array: The series of solar panels installed to capture sunlight for conversion into electricity or to heat hot water.

solar heat gain: Heat collected from the sun. This could be inside a room from direct sunlight, or held inside a material after absorption through sunlight.

sourcing: Finding sources that sell or provide green materials, products, and services. It also means examining the materials, products, and services to determine the true extent and nature of green practice. Sourcing applies to your café, shop, events, offices, exhibits, printers, promotions, and everything else.

stormwater runoff: The water from a rain event that does not immediately absorb into the ground but runs off in quantity. The water collects pollutants and debris from the surfaces that are harmful if discharged directly into water systems. The rate of discharge is also disruptive, creating erosion and altering natural water systems in ways that inhibit natural methods of cleaning and managing water flow. Usually the greatest amounts of stormwater runoff occur on impermeable surfaces: traditional roofs, walkways, driveways, and parking areas.

Target Finder: An Energy Star online tool for the design of projects, renovations, or new construction. It "helps architects and building owners set aggressive, realistic energy targets and rates a design's estimated energy use. The target and design ratings in Target Finder are derived from the Commercial Buildings Energy Consumption Survey (CBECS)." The website encourages using "Target Finder to achieve designs to earn the ENERGY STAR, which is required for participating in the ENERGY STAR Challenge.

Target Finder also helps you establish energy targets for Architecture 2030, which has been adopted by the American Institute of Architects and the U.S. Conference of Mayors."[5]

task lighting: A light source in the task area—a desk, workbench, or meeting table. This is more focused light than general overhead lighting. It allows individual users to turn lights off and on as needed without affecting others, and often results in reduced light use and therefore reduced electricity use.

thermal mass: Any material that has the capacity to store heat. How thermal mass is used in building construction depends on the climate. The classic application in the desert is adobe or rammed earth construction, where the thermal mass of the walls hold heat and restrict its flow from outside to inside during the day. At night the heat is released. In cold climates thermal mass is used in conjunction with passive solar design.

tree-free: Paper or products usually made from trees or wood products now made out of alternative substances expected to be environmentally sustainable.

triple bottom line (TBL): Calculating success based on three indicators (bottom lines): people, planet, and profit. The theory is that an institution's TBL should show positive effects for people, the environment, and income.

United States Green Building Council (USGBC): A nonprofit organization that was founded in 1993 by a group of architects, engineers, and construction experts to transform the way buildings are designed, built, and operated. The council is membership based and consensus driven and now includes over 10,000 member companies and organizations and a network of more than seventy local chapters, affiliates, and organizing groups.

variable frequency drive (VFD): Also known as adjustable frequency drives and variable speed drives. These drives save energy because the machines operate at the specific required demand of the system and cycle less frequently (using less energy) if the demand is lower.

volatile organic compounds (VOCs): An organic compound that evaporates at room temperature and contributes to poor indoor air quality. Museums have used low-VOC and zero-VOC finishes and materials in collection storage for years but a larger selection of low- and zero-VOC materials and style choices are now more available and more affordable.

walk-off mats: Mats, grates, or grids at the approach to a building that loosen and collect dirt, grit, and liquids as you walk across them, to prevent them from getting too far into your building. This focuses cleaning efforts on the entryway areas and not throughout the halls and rooms. It is far easier to clean a portable mat than to deep-clean permanent carpet; and it is greener to clean or replace one mat than to clean or replace much larger areas of carpet and floor.

Notes

1. www.energystar.gov/index.cfm?c=new_bldg_design.bus_target_finder, accessed January 20, 2008.

2. www.carbonfootprint.com/carbonfootprint.html, accessed December 14, 2007.

3. Many thanks to Aaron Binkley, AIA LEED AP, for this text on ESCOs.

4. www.energystar.gov/index.cfm?c=evaluate_performance.bus_portfoliomanager, accessed January 20, 2008.

5. www.energystar.gov/index.cfm?c=new_bldg_design.bus_target_finder, accessed January 20, 2008.

Index

About the Authors

Sarah S. Brophy is an independent consultant helping museums and other cultural institutions become environmentally and financially sustainable through grants, mainstreaming activities, and green performance. She is also a LEED-AP: a LEED-accredited professional through the U.S. Green Building Council.

Sarah has worked in museums in New England, the Mid-Atlantic, Colorado and Montana. After twenty years in Massachusetts, she now lives on the Eastern Shore of Maryland and is equally happy to be not-too-far from where she trained. She has a BA in American Studies from Sweet Briar College, an MA in history from the College of William & Mary, and a certificate in history administration from the William & Mary program with the Colonial Williamsburg Foundation. She is co-treasurer of the new Professional Interest Committee for AAM: PIC Green, and a member of the Green Buildings and Landscapes special section of the American Public Gardens and Association.

She and her family have embarked on their own green journey starting with recycling, cold-water-washed and line-hung laundry, and eschewing disposable shopping bags and coffee cups; they have moved on to successful composting, living in a walking town and owning only one car, and using the Boggle timer to monitor their three-minute showers. They each enjoy the journey to varying degrees.

Elizabeth Wylie has spent twenty years in the museum field as a curator and director and now directs business development activities for Finegold Alexander + Associates, a planning and architecture firm. Founded in the early 1960s, the firm is one of the pioneers in the historic preservation and adaptive use movement, and now specializes in sustainable design.

Elizabeth holds a BA in Art History from Boston University and a MA in Art History with a Certificate in Curatorial Studies from New York University's Institute of Fine Arts. She attended the Getty Leadership Institute (formerly MMI: Museum Management Institute) and taught in Tufts Museum Studies Program. She has held curatorial and administrative posts at art museums in New York, Massachusetts and Rhode Island and now volunteers at Fruitlands Museum and serves as Board president of the Jamaica Plain Tuesday Club, a 19th century women's club that stewards an 18th century historic house. Elizabeth is also, with Sarah, co-treasurer of the new Professional Interest Committee for AAM: PIC Green.

She has embraced mass transit in her commute to her job in downtown Boston and is actively making green changes to her home and lifestyle including water- and energy-efficiency measures in her arts and crafts house, buying local and recycled products, and walking whenever possible. She leads the green team at work and is helping her colleagues institute green office practices.

Together Sarah and Elizabeth have written "The Greener Good: The Enviro-Active Museum", *Museum*, Washington, D.C.: American Association of Museums, January/February 2008, and "It's Easy Being Green: Museums and the Green Movement", *Museum News*, Washington, D.C.: American Association of Museums, September/October 2006.